BIRDS *of* CHICAGO

Including NE Illinois & NW Indiana

Chris C. Fisher
David B. Johnson

LONE
PINE

First printed in 1998   10 9 8 7 6 5 4 3 2 1

Printed in Canada

The Publisher: Lone Pine Publishing

1901 Raymond Ave. SW, Suite C	206, 10426 – 81 Ave.	202A, 1110 Seymour St.
Renton, WA 98055	Edmonton, AB T6E 1X5	Vancouver, BC V6B 3N3
USA	Canada	Canada

Website: http://www.lonepinepublishing.com

Canadian Cataloguing in Publication Data

Fisher, Chris C. (Christopher Charles)
    Birds of Chicago

    Includes bibliographical references and index.
    ISBN 1-55105-112-5

    1. Birds—Illinois—Chicago—Identification. 2. Bird watching—Illinois—Chicago. I. Johnson, David B. (David Bruce), 1951– II. Title.
QL684.I3F57 1998   598'.09773'11   C97-910647-8

Senior Editor: Nancy Foulds
Project Editor: Roland Lines
Production Manager: David Dodge
Layout and Production: Michelle Bynoe
Cover Illustration: Gary Ross
Cartography: Volker Bodegom
Illustrations: Gary Ross, Ted Nordhagen, Ewa Pluciennik
Separations and Film: Elite Lithographers Co., Edmonton, Alberta
Printing: Quality Colour Press, Edmonton, Alberta

The checklist of Chicago-area birds (pp. 152–55) is reprinted from *Birds of the Greater Chicago Area: A Seasonal Checklist* with the kind permission of the Chicago Audubon Society. © 1982 Chicago Audubon Society, revised 1998.

The publisher gratefully acknowledges the assistance of the Department of Canadian Heritage.

Contents

Acknowledgments

A book such as this is made possible by the inspired work of Chicago's naturalist community and birding societies—the Chicago Audubon Society, Chicago Ornithological Society, Illinois Audubon Society, Illinois Ornithological Society and Evanston North Shore Bird Club, among others—which all make daily contributions to natural history, and whose contributions continue to advance the science of ornithology and to motivate a new generation of nature lovers.

My thanks go to Gary Ross and Ted Nordhagen, whose illustrations have elevated the quality of this book; to Carole Patterson, for her continual support; to the team at Lone Pine Publishing—Roland Lines, Nancy Foulds, Eloise Pulos, Michelle Bynoe and Shane Kennedy—for their input and steering; to John Acorn and Jim Butler, for their stewardship and their remarkable passion; and to Wayne Campbell, a premier naturalist whose works have served as models of excellence.

Chris C. Fisher

My thanks go to my mother, Jaynell, who encouraged me to be a summer camp naturalist for the Boy Scouts of America and who sent me my first bird tapes at camp (these I still have!); to Dad, Wib, who taught me my first bird call and who went on so many great birding adventures with me; and to my family, Jeri, Evan and Daren, who so graciously endure my birding obsessions. A special thanks must go to Larry Balch, who recommended that I take on this project; to Laurie Binford, Richard Biss, Lynne Carpenter, Charles T. Clark, Steven Mlodinow, James Neal, Joel Greenberg, Andy Sigler, Robert Hughes, Gerald Rosenband, Penny and Tom Pucelik, and Patti and Jim Ware, all of whom influenced my passion for birding. I must thank my late father-in-law, Dr. Samuel Pollack, who saw 'birds burnt into my retinas' and said someday I'd be involved in writing a bird book. He was right! Finally, I must thank the team of Lone Pine Publishing editors, publishers, proofreaders, writers and naturalists who suffered through my idiosyncracies.

David B. Johnson

Introduction

No matter where we live, birds are a natural part of our lives. We are so used to seeing them that we often take their presence for granted. When we take the time to notice their colors, songs and behaviors, we experience their dynamic appeal.

This book presents a brief introduction into the lives of birds. It is intended to serve as both a bird identification guide and a bird appreciation guide. Getting to know the names of birds is the first step toward getting to know birds. Once we've made contact with a species, we can better appreciate its character and mannerisms during future encounters. Over a lifetime of meetings, many birds become acquaintances, some seen daily, others not for years.

It would be impossible for a beginners' book such as this to comprehensively describe all the birds of the Chicago region. The selection of species within this book represents a balance between the familiar and the noteworthy. Many of the 126 species described in this guide are the most common species found in the Chicago area; others are less common, but they are noteworthy because they are important ecologically or because their particular status grants them a high profile. There is no one site where all the species in this book can be observed simultaneously, but most species can be viewed—at least seasonally—within a short drive from Chicago.

It is hoped that this guide will inspire novice birdwatchers into spending some time outdoors, gaining valuable experience with the local bird community. This book stresses the identity of birds, but it also attempts to bring them to life by discussing their various character traits. We often discuss a bird's character traits in human terms, because personifying a bird's character can help us to feel a bond with the birds. The perceived links with birds should not be mistaken for actual behaviors, as our interpretations can falsely reflect the complexities of bird life.

FEATURES OF THE LANDSCAPE

The variety of habitats around Chicago are home to a rich diversity of birds: more than 300 of our state's regularly occurring bird species have been found in and around our area. Situated along Lake Michigan and the Chicago River system, the Chicago area is a favorite spot for a wide variety of bird life.

The lakeshores and river valleys around Chicago act as natural pathways, funneling birds along their north-south migration routes. Stretches of beach and rocky shores strewn with pockets of shrubs and deciduous forests provide habitat and foraging opportunities for many birds. Along these shorelines, thousands of migrating geese, ducks, shorebirds, gulls and other birds stop to replenish their energy supplies, moving from one productive foraging site to another. Areas around Chicago's lakefront, such as Montrose Beach and Waukegan Harbor, are great for viewing waterfowl and other migrating birds in spring and fall. These waters remain open during winter, and many ducks and gulls can still be seen in our area.

Some of the most productive bird habitats are the inland lakes, sloughs and marsh areas common around the Chicago region. An abundance of plant and animal life attracts many migrating species, and during the breeding season, many birds build their nests along lakeshores or among the tall grasses and cattails of marshland edges. A visit to the McGinnis Slough or the lakes and marshes at Lake Calumet will inevitably offer rewarding birding opportunities: geese, grebes and ducks are common in these habitats, and during summer these wetlands are favored breeding spots for herons, egrets and coots.

Although most original prairie and grassland has disappeared from Illinois— the destruction of valuable habitat continues to be a significant factor contributing to a loss of bird life in our state—many prairie birds have adapted well to a new environment of pastures, woodland edges and roadside thickets. The hedgerows, edge habitats and uncultivated, grassy fields of the countryside provide shelter for a variety of migrant and nesting species. During spring and summer, look for sparrows, larks and blackbirds foraging for seeds and insects along open fields and roadsides. The fields and grassland areas of Illinois Beach State Park in Lake County offer unique year-round opportunities for the avid birder: during summer, these habitats provide nesting sites for many birds; in fall, great numbers of hawks can be seen passing overhead on their way south.

Broadleaf forests, including pockets of trees in backyards and city parks, are where you will find many of our songbirds. Every spring and fall, incredible numbers of woodland migrants funnel through our area, inundating local forest communities with exciting chatter and colorful song. At this time of year, areas such as Lincoln Park and the Swallow Cliff Forest Preserve become

Birdwatching Locations

1. Chain O'Lakes State Park
2. Illinois Beach State Park
3. Ryerson Conservation Area
4. Skokie Lagoons and the Chicago Botanic Garden
5. Gillson Park
6. Lincoln Park and the Montrose Harbor Area
7. Navy Pier
8. Jackson Park
9. Lake Calumet
10. Palos Area
11. Vollmer Road Area
12. Indiana Dunes State Park
13. Jasper-Pulaski State Fish and Wildlife Area

a bustling of activity as flycatchers, thrushes, vireos, warblers, sparrows and orioles take refuge in mixed stands of oak, maple, spruce and pine. Many warblers have endured exhausting flights on their migratory travels, and local woodlands provide much welcomed food, water and shelter. Wooded areas commonly found along streams, creeks and ponds are also favored habitat. A variety of species, including the Wood Duck, Warbling Vireo and Louisiana Waterthrush, rely on riparian habitats for feeding and sometimes for nest building.

The landscaped setting and rural neighborhoods of our city are also good places to become acquainted with bird life. Backyard feeders are a welcome invitation for many species during the colder months, and to the delight of area residents, many birds make use of nest boxes in summer. City parks and backyards are permanent homes for a long list of birds, including the Blue Jay, Cedar Waxwing, Northern Cardinal, American Goldfinch and a variety of woodpeckers. Urban development has also created new habitat for birds such as the Rock Dove, House Wren, European Starling and House Sparrow, which are exceptionally adapted to these settings and thrive in our human-made environment.

THE IMPORTANCE OF HABITAT

Understanding the relationships between habitats and bird species often helps identify which birds are which. Because you won't find a loon up a tree or a pheasant on a lake, habitat is an important thing to note when birdwatching.

The quality of habitat is one of the most powerful factors to influence bird distribution, and with experience you might become amazed by the predict-ability of some birds within a specific habitat type. The habitat icons in this book show where each species is most likely to be seen. It is important to real-ize, however, that because of their migratory habits, birds sometimes turn up in completely different habitats. These unexpected surprises, despite being confusing to novice birders, are among the most powerful motivations for the increasing legion of birdwatchers.

Lakes and
Open water

Shorelines

Marshes
and Wetlands

Parks and
Gardens

Fields and
Shrubby Areas

Coniferous
Forests

Broadleaf
Forests

THE ORGANIZATION OF THIS BOOK

To simplify field identification, *Birds of Chicago* is organized slightly differently from other field guides, many of which use strict phylogenetic groupings. In cases where many birds from the same family are described, conventional groupings are maintained in this book. In other cases, however, distantly related birds that share physical and behavioral similarities are grouped together. This blend of family groupings and groups of physically similar species strives to help the novice birdwatcher identify and appreciate the birds he or she encounters.

DIVING BIRDS

loons, grebes, cormorants

These heavy-bodied birds are adapted to diving for their food. Between their underwater foraging dives, they are most frequently seen on the surface of the water. These birds could only be confused with one another or with certain diving ducks.

WETLAND WADERS

herons, cranes, rails, coots

Although members of this group vary considerably in size and represent three separate families of birds, wetland waders share similar habitat and food preferences. Some of these long-legged birds are quite common in marshes, but certain species are heard far more than they are seen.

WATERFOWL

geese, ducks

Waterfowl tend to have stout bodies and webbed feet, and they are swift in flight. Although most species are associated with water, waterfowl can sometimes be seen grazing on upland sites.

VULTURES, HAWKS AND FALCONS

From deep forests to open country to large lakes, there are hawks and falcons hunting the skies. Their predatory look—sharp talons, hooked bills and forward-facing eyes—easily identifies members of this group. They generally forage during the day, and hawks and vultures use their broad wings to soar in thermals and updrafts.

PHEASANTS

These introduced Asian gamebirds bear a superficial resemblance to chickens. They are long, sleek birds and poor flyers, and they are most often encountered on the ground or when flushed.

SHOREBIRDS

plovers, sandpipers, woodcocks, etc.

Although these small, generally long-legged, swift-flying birds are mainly found along shores, don't be surprised to find some species in pastures and marshy areas.

GULLS AND TERNS

Gulls are relatively large, usually light-colored birds that are frequently seen swimming, walking about in urban areas or soaring gracefully over the city. Their backs tend to be darker than their bellies, and their feet are webbed. Terns are in the same family as gulls, but they rarely soar and they have straight, pointed bills.

DOVES AND PARROTS

Both of our doves are easily recognizable. Rock Doves are found in all urban areas, from city parks to the downtown core, but they have many of the same physical and behavioral characteristics as the 'wilder' Mourning Doves. The Monk Parakeet was introduced to Chicago from the jungles of South America.

NOCTURNAL BIRDS

owls, nightjars

These night hunters all have large eyes. Owls, which primarily prey on rodents, have powerful, taloned feet and strongly hooked bills. Nightjars, which catch moths and other nocturnal insects on the wing, have extremely large mouths.

KINGFISHERS

The Belted Kingfisher's behavior and physical characteristics are quite unlike any other bird's in Chicago. It primarily hunts fish, plunging after them from the air or from an overhanging perch.

WOODPECKERS

The drumming sound as they hammer wood and their precarious foraging habits easily identify most woodpeckers. They are frequently seen in forests, clinging to trunks and chipping away bark with their straight, sturdy bills. Even when these birds can't be seen or heard, you can find their characteristic marks on trees in any mature forest.

HUMMINGBIRDS

The Ruby-throated Hummingbird is Chicago's smallest bird. Its bright colors and swift flight are very characteristic.

FLYCATCHERS

wood-pewees, flycatchers, kingbirds

These birds might be best identified by their foraging behavior. As the name implies, flycatchers catch insects on the wing, darting after them from a favorite perch. Many flycatchers have subdued plumage, but kingbirds are rather boldly marked.

SWIFTS AND SWALLOWS

Members of these two families are typically seen at their nest sites or in flight. Small and sleek, swallows fly gracefully in pursuit of insects. Swifts are small, dark birds with long, narrow wings and short tails, and they have a more 'mechanical' flight behavior.

JAYS AND CROWS

Many members of this family are known for their intelligence and adaptability. These birds are easily observed, and they are often extremely bold, teasing the animal-human barrier. They are sometimes called 'corvids,' from Corvidae, the scientific name for the family.

SMALL SONGBIRDS

chickadees, wrens, kinglets, etc.

Birds in this group are all generally smaller than a sparrow. Many of them associate with one another in mixed-species flocks, and they are commonly encountered in city parks, backyards and other wooded areas.

BLUEBIRDS AND THRUSHES

bluebirds, thrushes, robins

From the bold robin to the secretive forest thrushes, this group of beautiful singers has the finest collective voice. Although some thrushes are very familiar, others require a little experience and patience to identify.

VIREOS AND WARBLERS

Vireos tend to dress in pale olive, whereas warblers are splashed liberally with colors. All these birds are very small, and they sing characteristic courtship songs, typically in woods and thickets.

MID-SIZED SONGBIRDS

tanagers, starlings, thrashers, etc.

The birds within this group are all sized between a sparrow and a robin. Tanagers are very colorful and sing complex, flute-like songs, but waxwings are more reserved in dress and voice. Starlings are frequently seen and heard all over the Chicago area.

SPARROWS

towhees, sparrows, juncos

These small, often indistinct birds are predominantly brown and streaky, and their songs are often very useful in identification. Many birdwatchers discount sparrows as 'little brown birds'—towhees are colorful exceptions—but they are worthy of the extra identification effort.

BLACKBIRDS AND ORIOLES

blackbirds, meadowlarks, cowbirds, etc.

Most of these birds are predominantly black and have relatively long tails. They are common in open areas, city parks and agricultural fields. The Eastern Meadowlark is also part of this family, despite not being black and having a short tail.

FINCH-LIKE BIRDS

finches, cardinals, grosbeaks, etc.

These finches and finch-like birds are primarily adapted to feeding on seeds, and they have stout, conical bills. Many are bird-feeder regulars, and they are a familiar part of the winter scene.

MEASUREMENTS

The size measurement given for each bird is an average length of the bird from the tip of its bill to the tip of its tail. It is an approximate measurement of the bird as it is seen in nature (rather than a measurement of stuffed specimens, which tend to be straighter and therefore longer).

In many situations, it is more useful to know a bird's comparative size, rather than its actual length in inches, so the 'Quick I.D.' for each species describes the bird's size in relation to a common, well-known bird (for example, sparrow-sized, smaller than a robin, etc.). It must be remembered that these are general impressions of size that are influenced as much by the bulk of a bird as by its total length.

PLUMAGES

One of the complications to birdwatching is that many species look different in spring and summer than they do in fall and winter—they have what are generally called *breeding* and *non-breeding* plumages—and young birds often look quite different from their parents. This book does not try to describe or illustrate all the different plumages of a species; instead, it focuses on the forms that are most commonly seen and are the easiest to identify in our area. All the illustrations are of adult birds.

ABUNDANCE CHARTS

Accompanying each bird description is a chart that indicates the relative abundance of the species throughout the year. These stylized graphs offer some insight

Jan Feb Mar Apr May Jun Jul Aug Sept Oct Nov Dec

into the distribution and abundance of the birds, but they should not be viewed as definitive—they represent a generalized overview. There could be inconsistencies specific to time and location, but these charts should provide readers with a basic reference for bird abundance and occurrence.

Each chart is divided into the 12 months of the year. The pale orange that colors the chart is an indication of abundance: the higher the color, the more common the bird. Dark orange is used to indicate the nesting period. The time frame is approximate, however, and nesting birds can sometimes be found both before and after the period indicated on the chart. If no nesting color is shown, the bird breeds outside the Chicago area, or it visits Chicago in significant numbers only during migration or winter.

These graphs are based on personal observations and on local references, including those listed on p. 151.

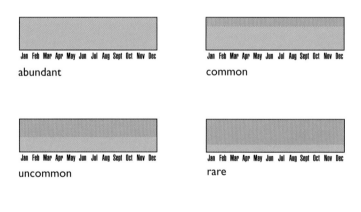

Jan Feb Mar Apr May Jun Jul Aug Sept Oct Nov Dec
abundant

Jan Feb Mar Apr May Jun Jul Aug Sept Oct Nov Dec
common

Jan Feb Mar Apr May Jun Jul Aug Sept Oct Nov Dec
uncommon

Jan Feb Mar Apr May Jun Jul Aug Sept Oct Nov Dec
rare

Jan Feb Mar Apr May Jun Jul Aug Sept Oct Nov Dec
unlikely

BIRDS *of* CHICAGO

Including NE Illinois & NW Indiana

Common Loon
Gavia immer

The Common Loon is a symbol of northern wilderness, preferring the diminishing pristine areas where birds alone quarrel over boreal wetlands. They do not breed in our area, but visit Chicago each year during migration. Listen for their primeval wilderness voice during spring, when passing birds practice their courting songs. Their intricate, almost reptilian, dark green–and–white breeding plumage can be seen in spring among the 80-plus glacial lakes in Lake County or off Lake Michigan's shoreline as the birds wait for the ice to melt on interior lakes. In fall, loons can best be seen migrating offshore or floating in the waters off Illinois Beach State Park and Navy Pier.

Loons routinely poke their heads underwater, spotting potential prey and plotting their forthcoming pursuit. They dive deeply and efficiently, compressing their feathers to reduce underwater drag and to decrease their buoyancy. Propelling themselves primarily with their legs, these birds can outswim some fish over short distances. Because they have solid bones (unlike most other birds) and because their legs are placed well back on their bodies for diving, Common Loons require long stretches of open water for take-off.

Similar Species: Common Merganser (p. 40) has a red bill and very white plumage. Double-crested Cormorant (p. 20) has all-black plumage, a long neck and an orange bill, and it usually holds its head pointed upward when it swims. Red-throated Loon is smaller and has a slimmer bill and a rounded head.

breeding

Quick I.D.: larger than a duck; sexes similar; stout, long, dagger-like bill. *Breeding:* dark green-black hood; black-and-white checkerboard back; fine, black-and-white 'necklace.' *Non-breeding:* sandy-brown back; whitish underparts. *In flight:* hunchbacked.
Size: 27–33 in.

Jan Feb Mar Apr May Jun Jul Aug Sept Oct Nov Dec

Pied-billed Grebe
Podilymbus podiceps

The small, stout, drab body of the Pied-billed Grebe seems perfectly suited to its marshy habitat, but its loud, whooping *kuk-kuk-cow-cow-cow-cowp-cowp* is a sound that seems more at home in tropical rainforests. Pied-billed Grebes can be found on most freshwater wetlands that are surrounded by cattails, bulrushes or other emergent vegetation. These diving birds are frustrating to follow as they disappear and then reappear, with only their heads appearing above the water's surface.

During summer, these small, reclusive grebes often nest within view of lakeside trails. They build nests that float on the water's surface, and their eggs often rest in waterlogged vegetation. Young grebes take their first swim soon after hatching, but they will instinctively clamber aboard a parent's back at the first sign of danger.

Similar Species: Ducks have bills that are flattened top to bottom. Horned Grebe and Eared Grebe have light underparts.

breeding

Jan Feb Mar Apr May Jun Jul Aug Sept Oct Nov Dec

Quick I.D.: smaller than a duck; sexes similar; all brown. *Breeding:* dark vertical band on thick, pale, blue-gray bill; black chin. *First-year (summer/fall):* striped brown and white.
Size: 12–14 in.

Double-crested Cormorant
Phalacrocorax auritus

When Double-crested Cormorants fly in single-file, low over Lake Michigan, the prehistoric sight hints to their ancestry. The tight, dark flocks soar over lakes, until hunger or the need for rest draws them to the water's surface. It is there that cormorants are most comfortable, disappearing beneath the surface in deep foraging dives or resting atop the water.

Cormorants lack the ability to waterproof their feathers, so they need to dry their wings after each swim. These large, black waterbirds are frequently seen perched on dead trees, piers or jetties, with their wings partially spread to expose their wet feathers to the sun and the wind. It would seem to be a great disadvantage for a waterbird to have to dry its wings, but the cormorant's ability to wet its feathers decreases its buoyancy, making it easier for it to swim after the fish on which it preys. Sealed nostrils, a long, rudder-like tail and excellent underwater vision are other features of the Double-crested Cormorant's aquatic lifestyle.

Similar Species: Common Loon (p. 18) has a shorter neck and is more stout overall.

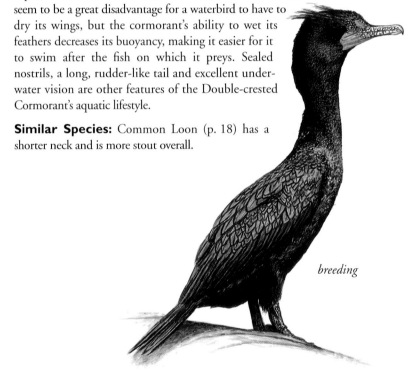

breeding

Quick I.D.: goose-sized; sexes similar; all black; long tail; long neck. *Breeding:* bright orange bill and throat pouch; black plumes streaming back from eyebrows (seen only at close range). *First-year:* brown; pale neck, breast and belly. *In flight:* kinked neck; rapid wingbeats.
Size: 30–35 in.

Jan Feb Mar Apr May Jun Jul Aug Sept Oct Nov Dec

Great Blue Heron
Ardea herodias

breeding

The Great Blue Heron is one of the largest and most noticed herons in our area. It often stands motionless as it surveys the calm waters, its graceful lines blending naturally with the grasses and cattails of wetlands. All herons have specialized vertebrae that enable the neck to fold back over itself. The S-shaped neck, seen in flight, identifies all members of this wading family.

Hunting herons space themselves out evenly in favorite hunting spots, and they will strike out suddenly at prey below the water's surface. In flight, their lazy wingbeats slowly but effortlessly carry them up to their nests. These herons nest communally, high in trees, building bulky stick nests that are sometimes in plain sight of urban areas. Almost any wetland produces good views of this bird, which is common in spring, summer and fall and uncommon in winter.

Similar Species: None.

Jan Feb Mar Apr May Jun Jul Aug Sept Oct Nov Dec

Quick I.D.: very large heron; eagle-sized wing-span; sexes similar; red thighs; long, dagger-like, yellow bill. *In flight:* head folded back; legs held straight back.
Size: 48–52 in.

Green Heron
Butorides virescens

This crow-sized heron is far less conspicuous than its Great Blue cousin. The Green Heron prefers to hunt for frogs and small fish in shallow, weedy wetlands, where it is often seen perched just above the water's surface. By searching the shallow, shady, overgrown wetland edges around lakes, rivers and open marshes, Chicago's birders can get a prolonged view of this reclusive bird.

The Green Heron often uses all of its stature to hunt over a favorite site. With its bright yellow feet clasping a branch or reed, this small heron stretches nearly horizontally over the water, its pose rigid and unchanging, until a fish swims into range. Like a taut bowstring, the tension mounts until the heron chooses to fire. Lunging its entire body at the prey, it is often soaked to the shoulders following a successful hunt.

Similar Species: Black-crowned Night-Heron (p. 23) is larger and has light underparts. American Bittern is larger and heavily streaked, and lacks any green color.

Quick I.D.: crow-sized; sexes similar; small, stubby heron; short legs; glossy green back; chestnut nape and throat; dark cap. *Breeding male:* orange legs. *Immature:* less colorful, with more streaking in throat and breast.
Size: 18–21 in.

Jan Feb Mar Apr May Jun Jul Aug Sept Oct Nov Dec

Black-crowned Night-Heron
Nycticorax nycticorax

breeding

As daylight fades, a distinctive *wok-wok* call announces a flock of Black-crowned Night-Herons flying to a marsh to feed. These birds prefer to feed at this time of day, and their shapes can be among the last forms visible in summer's golden evening light. These white-plumed, pony-tailed birds possess remarkably large eyes, a possible advantage in their nocturnal foraging efforts.

Black-crowned Night-Herons are much more difficult to find in the middle of the day, because they roost inconspicuously in shoreline vegetation. They nest in low bushes, and have generally become increasingly uncommon in our area in the past decades. The degradation and destruction of vital wetlands have resulted in a sharp decline in this bird's abundance, and it has been included on the Illinois State Endangered Species List. The Black-crowned Night-Heron is one of the world's most abundant and widespread herons, so its endangered status in Illinois strongly signals the state's dire need for increased wetland conservation.

Similar Species: Great Blue Heron (p. 21) is larger and has a long neck. Green Heron (p. 22) has a greenish-black cap, a chestnut neck and greenish upperparts. American Bittern is similar to a juvenile night-heron, but it has black wing tips and a black mustache stripe. Yellow-crowned Night-Heron has a white cheek patch and crown.

Quick I.D.: mid-sized heron; sexes similar; black crown and back; gray neck and wings; white cheek and belly; moderately long legs. *Breeding:* white plumes from back of head. *Juvenile:* brown; heavily streaked and spotted. **Size:** 24–26 in.

Jan Feb Mar Apr May Jun Jul Aug Sept Oct Nov Dec

Sandhill Crane
Grus canadensis

The Sandhill Crane's deep, rolling, guttural rattle announces the presence of a migrating flock long before the birds can be seen on the horizon. The loud chorus—*ga-rooo ga-rooo!*—precedes the high-flying birds and alerts attentive naturalists to one of Illinois's most marvelous spectacles. During migration, Sandhill Cranes pass over the Jasper-Pulaski State Fish and Wildlife Area by the thousands.

Sandhill Cranes are among the largest of the birds that can be seen in our area. They stand as high as a pre-teenage child, they have a wing-span the height of a professional basketball player, and they have a voice matched only by the most powerful of opera singers. Occasionally, during spring and fall, a flock might land on surrounding farmlands in our area. There they feast on waste grain and corn before continuing on their voyage. The sights and sounds of these great birds enable urban residents to connect vicariously to far-off wilderness areas.

Similar Species: Great Blue Heron (p. 21) flies with its neck arched over its shoulders and lacks the red forehead patch.

Quick I.D.: very large bird; sexes similar; pale gray plumage; long, slender neck; long, thin, dark legs; naked red crown; long, straight bill; plumage often stained rusty from iron oxides in water. *Juvenile:* no red patch; light plumage with patches of orange-red. *In flight:* neck fully extended; legs extended; slow downbeat; quick upstroke.
Size: 41–47 in.

Jan Feb Mar Apr May Jun Jul Aug Sept Oct Nov Dec

Sora
Porzana carolina

Skulking around freshwater marshes in the Chicago area is the seldom-seen Sora. Although this rail arrives in good numbers in spring, it is not a species that can be encountered with any predictability. Visual meetings with the Sora in Chicago arise unexpectedly, usually when birdwatchers are out in good wetlands searching for less reclusive species. At other times this bird unexpectedly shows up in a bush along the waterfront, such as in the Magic Hedge at the Montrose Promontory. Although it has declined in our area, its loud call, *So-ra, So-ra,* followed by a descending whinny, can still be heard at many area marshes.

Urban sprawl and agricultural expansion have come at the expense of many Chicago birds. The Sora's marshland habitat is often thought to be unproductive by human standards, but these shallow, nutrient-rich wetlands host a bounty of wildlife. With the growing legion of birdwatchers and nature lovers, societal values might finally shift toward an understanding of our natural communities and wetland protection.

Similar Species: Virginia Rail has a long, reddish, downcurved bill.

breeding

Jan Feb Mar Apr May Jun Jul Aug Sept Oct Nov Dec

Quick I.D.: robin-sized; sexes similar; short, yellow bill; front of face is black; gray neck and breast; long, greenish legs.
Size: 8–10 in.

American Coot
Fulica americana

The American Coot is a mix of comedy and confusion: it seems to have been made up of bits and pieces leftover from other birds. It has the lobed toes of a grebe, the bill of a chicken and the body shape and swimming habits of a duck, but it is not remotely related to any of these species: its closest cousins are rails and cranes. American Coots dabble and dive in water and forage on land, and they eat both plant and animal matter. They can be found in just about every freshwater pond, lake, marsh, lagoon or city park in Chicago, and during migration they can number in the thousands.

These loud, grouchy birds are seen chugging along in wetlands, frequently entering into short-lived disputes with other coots. American Coots appear comical while they swim: their heads bob in time with their paddling feet, and as a coot's swimming speed increases, so does the back-and-forth motion of its head. At peak speed, this motion seems to disorient the coot, so it prefers to run, flap and splash to the other side of the wetland.

Similar Species: All ducks and grebes generally lack the uniform black color and the white bill.

Quick I.D.: smaller than a duck; sexes similar; black body; white bill; red forehead shield; short tail; long legs; lobed feet; white undertail coverts.
Size: 14–16 in.

Jan Feb Mar Apr May Jun Jul Aug Sept Oct Nov Dec

Canada Goose
Branta canadensis

Most flocks of Canada Geese in city parks and golf courses show little concern for their human neighbors. These urban geese seem to think nothing of creating a traffic jam, blocking a fairway or dining on lawns and gardens. Their love of manicured parks and gardens and the lack of predators have created a population explosion in the Chicago area.

Breeding pairs of Canada Geese are regal in appearance and their loyalty is legendary—they mate for life, and it's common for a mate to stay at the side of a fallen partner. Canada Geese are common throughout the Chicago area during every season of the year.

Similar Species: None.

Jan Feb Mar Apr May Jun Jul Aug Sept Oct Nov Dec

Quick I.D.: large goose; sexes similar; white cheek; black head and neck; brown body; white undertail coverts.
Size: 35–42 in.

Wood Duck
Aix sponsa

Only days old, small Wood Duck ducklings are lured out of the only world they know by their pleading mother. Although this seems typical of most ducks, young Wood Ducks require more coaxing than most—their nest is an old woodpecker hole high in a tree. With a faith-filled leap, the cottonball ducklings tumble toward the ground, often bouncing on impact. When all the siblings have leapt into the waiting world, they follow their mother through the dense underbrush to the nearest water.

Many of the old, rotten, hollow lakeside trees that provided excellent nesting sites for Wood Ducks have diminished in the Chicago area. As a result, more and more young Wood Ducks are beginning life by tumbling out of nest boxes made by humans. The Wood Ducks are provided with a secure nest site in which to incubate their eggs, while landowners have the honor of having North America's most handsome ducks living on their land. The male Wood Duck is one of the continent's most colorful birds; no other duck can match his much-celebrated, iridescent, colorful and intricate plumage.

Similar Species: Male is very distinctive. Female resembles many other small, female ducks, but has a prominent, wide, white eye ring.

Quick I.D.: small duck. *Male:* glossy green head; crest slicked back from crown; white chin and throat; chestnut breast spotted white; white shoulder slash; golden sides; dark back and hindquarters. *Female:* white teardrop eye patch; mottled brown breast streaked white; brown-gray upperparts; white belly.
Size: 18–20 in.

Jan Feb Mar Apr May Jun Jul Aug Sept Oct Nov Dec

American Wigeon
Anas americana

During spring and fall migration, American Wigeons can easily be found and identified in the sloughs of Chicago's flooded fields and lakes. Flocks of wigeons waddle across lawns at Gillson Park or Waukegan Harbor, begging scraps intended for pigeons. The white top and gray sides of the male American Wigeon's head look somewhat like a balding scalp, while the nasal *wee-he-he-he* calls sound remarkably like the squeaks of a squeezed rubber ducky.

Although they breed to the north and winter primarily on the Atlantic, American Wigeons are becoming increasingly visible in our area during their passage. At this time of year hundreds can be seen in such areas as Lake Calumet, refueling for the continuation of their trip.

Similar Species: Green-winged Teal is smaller and has a white shoulder slash and a rusty head with a green swipe.

Jan Feb Mar Apr May Jun Jul Aug Sept Oct Nov Dec

Quick I.D.: mid-sized duck; cinnamon breast and flanks; white belly; gray bill with black tip; green speculum. *Male:* white forehead; green swipe running back from eye. *Female:* no distinct color on head.
Size: 18–21 in.

American Black Duck
Anas rubripes

Among the flocks of waterfowl wintering on open water in the Chicago area, you will find the plain-looking American Black Duck. Like a dark version of the familiar Mallard (except for its silver wing linings, dark orange feet and purple wing patch), the American Black Duck is the classic duck of eastern North America, traditionally having a stronghold throughout the Great Lakes states.

Unfortunately the eastern expansion of Mallards has come at the expense of this dark dabbler. As its green-headed cousin spread into our area, the American Black Duck quickly hybridized with the Mallard. This genetic watering down of pure American Black Duck stock has concerned biologists, and the future stability of this species is unknown. Habitat loss and the degradation of wetlands in general have further contributed to the decline of this bird. Although plain in appearance, the state of the American Black Duck's future increases its profile in the eyes and minds of conservation-oriented naturalists.

Similar Species: Mallard (p. 31) has an overall lighter body plumage and a blue speculum, and the male has a green head.

Quick I.D.: large duck; dark blackish-brown body; light brown head and neck; violet speculum; bright orange feet. *Male:* yellow bill. *Female:* dull green bill spotted with black. *In flight:* silver-lined wings.
Size: 22–24 in.

Mallard

Anas platyrhynchos

The Mallard is the urban duck of the Chicago area—the male's iridescent green head and chestnut breast make this bird easy to identify. This large duck is commonly seen feeding in city parks, small lakes and shallow bays, or in cornfields alongside Canada Geese. With its legs positioned under the middle part of its body, the Mallard walks easily, and it can spring straight out of the water without a running start.

Mallards are the most common duck in North America (and the Northern Hemisphere), and they are easily seen year-round in Chicago. During winter, Mallards are seen banding together in loose flocks in any open water. Birdwatchers habitually scan these groups to test their identification skills. Mallards (like all ducks) molt their feathers, so remember that the distinctive green head of the male Mallard occasionally loses its green pizzazz.

Similar Species: Female resembles many other female dabbling ducks, but look for the blue speculum and her close association with the male Mallard. Male Northern Shoveler (p. 33) has a green head, a white breast and chestnut flanks.

Jan Feb Mar Apr May Jun Jul Aug Sept Oct Nov Dec

Quick I.D.: large duck; bright orange feet; blue speculum bordered by white. *Male:* iridescent green head; bright yellow bill; chestnut breast; white flanks. *Female:* mottled brown; bright orange bill marked with black.
Size: 22–26 in.

Blue-winged Teal
Anas discors

The male Blue-winged Teal has a thin, white crescent on his cheek and a steel blue-gray head to match his inner wing patches. These small ducks are extremely swift flyers, which frustrates their many predators. Their sleek design and rapid wingbeats enable teals to swerve, even at great speeds, and also provide the small ducks the accuracy to make perfectly placed landings. Unlike many ducks that nest pondside, Blue-winged Teals often nest far from water on upland prairies and fallow fields.

Unlike many of the larger dabblers that overwinter in the United States, teals migrate to Central and South America. For this reason, the Blue-winged Teal is often the last duck to arrive in Chicago during spring and the first to leave in fall, usually by the end of September.

Similar Species: Female is easily confused with other female ducks.

Quick I.D.: very small duck; blue forewing; green speculum. *Male:* steel blue head; white crescent on cheek. *Female:* small; plain; yellow-orange legs.
Size: 14–16 in.

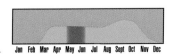

Northern Shoveler
Anas clypeata

When people start birdwatching, one of their first realizations is that several ducks sport green heads. Other than the Mallard, the Northern Shoveler is one of the easiest to identify—the Northern Shoveler's shovel-like bill stands out among dabbling ducks. The comb-like structures along the bill's edges and its broad, flat shape allow the shoveler to strain small plants and invertebrates from the water's surface or from muddy substrates. A few Northern Shovelers breed in the Chicago area, but most breed farther west.

Many novice birders become interested in birds because they realize the great variety of ducks in their city parks. Some ducks, like the Northern Shoveler, are dabblers that prefer shallow water, are not opposed to roaming around on land and lift straight off the water like a helicopter. Many other ducks in the Chicago area are divers that are found on large lakes. They can be seen running across the water to gain enough speed for flight. Separating the divers from the dabblers is a first step into the wondrous world of waterfowl.

Similar Species: Mallard (p. 31) and all other dabbling ducks lack the combination of a large bill, a white breast and chestnut brown sides.

Jan Feb Mar Apr May Jun Jul Aug Sept Oct Nov Dec

Quick I.D.: mid-sized duck; large bill (longer than head width). *Male:* green head; white breast; chestnut sides. *Female:* mottled brown overall.
Size: 18–20 in.

Ring-necked Duck
Aythya collaris

During the peak of waterfowl migration, Ring-necked Ducks can be quite common on Lake Michigan and all inland lakes. These diving ducks prefer ponds and lakes with muddy bottoms—they dive deeply underwater for aquatic vegetation, including seeds, tubers and pondweed leaves, and invertebrates. Because of their foraging habits, Ring-necked Ducks are susceptible to poisoning from ingesting lead shot. (Wasted shotgun pellets lie at the bottom of many rural wetlands and throughout this duck's summer range across the northern states and Canada.)

Although this duck's name implies the presence of a collar, most experienced birders have given up on seeing this faint feature. The only prominent ring noticeable in field observations is around the tip of the bill, suggesting that a more reasonable name for this bird would have been 'Ring-billed Duck.'

Similar Species: Lesser Scaup (p. 35) and Greater Scaup lack the white shoulder slash and the black back. Female Redhead has a dark brown head to match its body.

Quick I.D.: mid-sized duck; black bill tip; white bill ring. *Male:* dark head with hints of purple; black breast, back and hindquarters; white shoulder slash; gray sides; blue-gray bill with prominent white ring around base. *Female:* dark brown body; light brown head; white eye ring; lighter color closer to bill.
Size: 16–18 in.

Jan Feb Mar Apr May Jun Jul Aug Sept Oct Nov Dec

Lesser Scaup
Aythya affinis

The Lesser Scaup is the Oreo cookie of the duck world—black at both ends and white in the middle. It is a diving duck that prefers deep, open water, and it is common on lakes, harbors and lagoons. As a result of its diving adaptations, the Lesser Scaup is clumsy on land and during take-off, but it gains dignity when it takes to the water. For close-up views, visit the Chicago Botanic Garden or any inland lake in our area.

Because of Chicago's location on Lake Michigan, most species of ducks here are of the diving variety, even though the dabblers are often the most frequently encountered. Diving ducks have smaller wings, which help them dive underwater but make for difficult take-offs and landings. If a duck scoots across the water in an attempt to get airborne, even a first-time birder can tell it's a diver. Divers' legs are placed well back on their bodies—an advantage for underwater swimming—so in order for diving ducks to stand, they must raise their heavy front ends high to maintain balance.

Similar Species: Ring-necked Duck (p. 34) has a white shoulder slash and a black back. Greater Scaup has a green tinge to its head and a long, white stripe on the trailing edge of its wing (seen in flight), and its head lacks the 'bump' on the back of its crown.

Jan Feb Mar Apr May Jun Jul Aug Sept Oct Nov Dec

Quick I.D.: small duck; peaked head. *Male:* dark head with hints of purple; black breast and hindquarters; dirty white sides; grayish back; bluegray bill; no white breast slash. *Female:* dark brown; well-defined white patch at base of bill. **Size:** 15–17 in.

Oldsquaw
Clangula hyemalis

♂

winter

♀

Oldsquaws are tough ducks, lingering in the Chicago area during the harshest time of year—winter. They stop over on Lake Michigan from fall through early spring, during which time their seasonal dress is completely transformed like a photo-negative. The spring breeding plumage of these Arctic-nesting sea ducks is mostly dark with white highlights, while the winter plumage— most frequently seen on our waters—features the opposing characteristics. Regardless of their color, these handsome ducks usually frequent Lake Michigan in rafts a mile or more offshore, limiting observers to brief glimpses of their long, slender tail feathers from Navy Pier, Gillson Park and Waukegan and Racine harbors.

Oldsquaws are among the noisiest breeders on the tundra, their voice is often used to audibly define the Arctic during summer. During their stay here the birds are also vocal, giving the people unable to travel north a taste of Arctic summers. While foraging for minnows, crustaceans and mollusks, Oldsquaws calmly dive to the bottom of our lakes for up to 30 seconds. They are well suited to our winter weather, and the icy pearls of water slide off the bird's body once it resurfaces.

Similar Species: None.

Quick I.D.: mid-sized duck; male has long tail feathers. *Winter male:* white head, flanks, back and underparts; dark cheek, breast and wings. *Winter female:* dark back; light underparts. *Summer male:* dark head, back and neck; white cheek and underparts; pink bill with black base and tip. *Summer female:* light flanks and head; dark cheek.
Size: 17–20 in.

Jan Feb Mar Apr May Jun Jul Aug Sept Oct Nov Dec

Bufflehead
Bucephala albeola

The small, fluffy Bufflehead is perhaps the 'cutest' of Chicago's ducks: its simple plumage and rotund physique bring to mind a child's stuffed toy. During winter, a few Buffleheads are found on just about every lake, particularly off rocky jetties and piers on Lake Michigan.

Because ducks spend most of their lives dripping with water, preening is an important behavior. At the base of the tail of most birds lies the preen (uropygial) gland, which secretes a viscous liquid that inhibits bacterial growth and waterproofs and conditions the feathers. After gently squeezing the preen gland with its bill, a bird can spread the secretion methodically over most of its body, an essential practice to revitalize precious feathers. Sun and wind damage feathers, so it is understandable that birds spend so much time in the preening and maintenance of their feathers.

Similar Species: Male Common Goldeneye (p. 38) is larger and lacks the white, unbordered triangle behind the eye, and the female has a brown head and lacks the cheek patch.

Jan Feb Mar Apr May Jun Jul Aug Sept Oct Nov Dec

Quick I.D.: tiny duck; round body. *Male:* white triangle on back of dark head; white body; dark back. *Female:* dirty brown overall; small, white cheek patch.
Size: 13–15 in.

Common Goldeneye
Bucephala clangula

Although Common Goldeneyes don't breed in the Chicago area, these 'ice ducks' are very common from late fall, through the freezing winter, and right up to their spring migration. Their courtship antics, staged on Lake Michigan and just about every other large waterbody from winter through spring, reinforce a pair's bond before their migration to Canadian woodland lakes.

The courtship display of this widespread duck is one of nature's best slapstick routines. The spry male goldeneye rapidly arches his large, green head back until his bill points skyward, producing a seemingly painful *kraaaagh!* Completely unaffected by this chiropractic wonder, he continuously performs this ritual to mainly disinterested females. The male escalates his spring performance, creating a comedic scene that is most appreciated by birdwatchers.

Similar Species: Bufflehead (p. 37) and Hooded Merganser lack the round, white cheek patch.

Quick I.D.: mid-sized duck. *Male:* large, dark green to black head; round, white cheek patch; white body; black back streaked with white. *Female:* chocolate brown hood; sandy-colored body; orange-brown bill.
Size: 17–19 in.

Jan Feb Mar Apr May Jun Jul Aug Sept Oct Nov Dec

Red-breasted Merganser
Mergus serrator

During spring, Red-breasted Mergansers congregate near the shores of Lake Michigan, initiating their courting rituals prior to their final push north. Males, with their punk-like, slicked crests, ride on the waters while lowering their necks under the surface. With their mid-points submerged, these ducks stare eerily with their wild red eyes, evaluating the females' responses to their actions.

Large, gregarious flocks of Red-breasted Mergansers visit the Great Lakes during migration. However, unlike Common Mergansers, they tend to retreat to coastal waters for winter. During their stay in our waters, their quick 'fly bys' and flashing, white inner wing patches are common features off any lakefront park.

Similar Species: Male Common Merganser (p. 40) lacks the red breast and has white underparts, and the female has a well-defined, reddish-brown hood. Other large ducks and Common Loon (p. 18) all lack the combination of a green head, red bill, red feet and brownish breast.

Quick I.D.: large duck; gray body. *Male:* well-defined, dark green hood; punk-like crest; breast speckled with light brown and black; white collar; brilliant reddish bill and feet; black spinal streak. *Female:* rusty hood blending into white chest.
Size: 21–25 in.

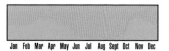

Jan Feb Mar Apr May Jun Jul Aug Sept Oct Nov Dec

Common Merganser

Mergus merganser

Laboring like a large jumbo jet trying to take off, the Common Merganser runs along the surface of the water, beating its heavy wings until sufficient speed is reached for lift-off. Once in the air, our largest duck looks compressed and arrow-like as it flies strongly in low, straight lines over rivers and lakes.

Mergansers are lean and powerful waterfowl, designed for the underwater pursuit of fish. Unlike the bills of other fish-eating birds, the bill of a merganser is saw-like, serrated to ensure that its squirmy, slimy prey does not escape. In Chicago, Common Mergansers are seen during migration and in winter, when these large ducks congregate in rafts in areas of open water at the mouth of the Chicago River.

Similar Species: Common Loon (p. 18) has a straight dark bill and darker sides. Red-breasted Merganser (p. 39) lacks the white breast and sides.

Quick I.D.: goose-sized. *Male:* well-defined, dark green hood; white body; brilliant reddish-orange bill and feet; black spinal streak.
Female: rusty hood; clean white throat and chin; gray body.
Size: 23–26 in.

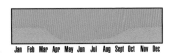

Jan Feb Mar Apr May Jun Jul Aug Sept Oct Nov Dec

Ruddy Duck
Oxyura jamaicensis

♀ ♂

breeding

The clowns of freshwater wetlands, male Ruddy Ducks energetically paddle around their breeding wetlands, displaying with great vigor and beating their breasts with their bright blue beaks. The *plap-plap-plap-plap-plap* sound of their display speeds up until its climax: a spasmodic jerk and sputter. The male's performance occurs from April to the middle of June and can occasionally be seen on upland lakes.

Unfortunately, most Ruddy Ducks seen in the Chicago area do not remain to breed. Most courting birds observed in our area continue north to find suitable nesting areas. These birds, however, return in fall and are easily identified not by color but by their unique shape and habits. At this time of year, even the male Ruddy Ducks have lost their ruddy plumage and blue bill, but they maintain their cocky disposition, which seems to be expressed through their permanent smile.

Similar Species: All other waterfowl are generally larger and have shorter tails, relatively smaller heads and longer necks.

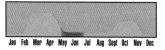

Jan Feb Mar Apr May Jun Jul Aug Sept Oct Nov Dec

Quick I.D.: small duck; broad bill; large head; tail often cocked up. *Breeding male:* reddish-brown neck and body; black head and tail; white cheek; blue bill. *Non-breeding male:* dull brown overall; dark cap; white cheek. *Female:* like non-breeding male, but cheek has a dark stripe. **Size:** 14–16 in.

Turkey Vulture
Cathartes aura

Soaring effortlessly above our river valleys and agricultural lands, Turkey Vultures ride rising thermals during their afternoon foraging flights. They seldom need to flap their silver-lined wings, and they rock gently from side to side as they carefully scan fields and shorelines for carcasses. Even at great distances, this bare-headed bird can be identified by the way it tends to hold its wings upwards in a shallow 'V.'

The Turkey Vulture feeds entirely on carrion, which it can sometimes detect by scent alone. Its head is featherless, which is an adaptation to staying clean and parasite-free while it roots around inside carcasses. This king scavenger's well-known habit of regurgitating its rotting meal at intruders might be a defense mechanism: it allows Turkey Vultures to reduce their weight for a quicker take-off, and its smell helps young vultures repel would-be predators.

Similar Species: Hawks, eagles and the Osprey have large, feathered heads and tend to hold their wings flatter in flight, not in a shallow 'V.'

Quick I.D.: larger than a hawk; sexes similar; all black; small, red head. *Immature:* black head. *In flight:* wings held in a shallow 'V'; silver-gray flight feathers; dark wing linings; rocks side to side.
Size: 27–30 in.

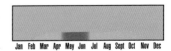

Jan Feb Mar Apr May Jun Jul Aug Sept Oct Nov Dec

Cooper's Hawk
Accipiter cooperii

If songbirds dream, the Cooper's Hawk is sure to be the source of their nightmares: Cooper's Hawks terrorize the songbirds living in Chicago's neighborhoods. This mid-sized raptor pursues small birds through forests, maneuvering around leaves and branches in the hope of acquiring prey. Cooper's Hawks take more birds than other accipiters, with small songbirds and the occasional woodpecker being the most numerous prey items.

These small hawks are easy to find darting through European Starling flocks as they pass through our area during their spring and fall migration. During winter, a few of Chicago's wooded neighborhoods have a resident Cooper's Hawk, eager to capture unwary doves, starlings and cardinals. Backyard feeders tend to concentrate favored prey, so they are attractive foraging areas for this small hawk. A sudden eruption of birds off the feeder and a few feathers floating on the wind are often the signs of a sudden, successful Cooper's attack.

Similar Species: Sharp-shinned Hawk is usually smaller, and its tail is squared off and has a thin terminal band. Northern Goshawk is much larger and has white eyebrows.

Quick I.D.: smaller than a crow; sexes similar; short, round wings; long tail; blue-gray back; rusty horizontal streaking on underparts; red eyes. *Immature:* brown overall; vertical, brown breast streaks; yellow eyes. *In flight:* flap-and-glide flyer; heavily barred tail is rounded at white tip. **Size:** 15–19 in. (female larger).

Jan Feb Mar Apr May Jun Jul Aug Sept Oct Nov Dec

Broad-winged Hawk
Buteo platypterus

Sighting this mid-sized hawk is a hit-and-miss affair. It is fairly secretive in its wooded breeding habitat, and summers often produce precious few breeding pairs. During migration, however, certain areas, such as the Des Plaines River valley, can produce thousands in a single day! These inconsistencies in observation are not restricted solely to this species, but the Broad-winged Hawk might be the best example of a bird that both frustrates and rewards persistent birders.

Hawks' heavy wings are not designed for continual flapping flight, so these raptors seek out areas that reduce their need to flap. Lake Michigan and the other Great Lakes are daunting to Broad-winged Hawks, which prefer to skirt around the edges, funneling through areas that provide welcome updrafts. Migrating raptors seek out rising thermals created by warm air, or air currents deflecting up from cliffs. The currents help them gain elevation before they launch across a stretch of stagnant, heavy air, giving them longer glides.

Similar Species: Red-tailed Hawk (p. 45) has a solid red tail. Cooper's Hawk (p. 43) has a long, narrow tail. Rough-legged Hawk is a winter visitor. Red-shouldered Hawk has rusty under wings and tail.

Quick I.D.: smaller than a crow; sexes similar; wide white bands on black, fan-like tail; horizontal russet barring on chest; short, rounded wings; black wing tips.
Size: 15–17 in.

Jan Feb Mar Apr May Jun Jul Aug Sept Oct Nov Dec

Red-tailed Hawk
Buteo jamaicensis

With its fierce facial expression and untidy feathers, the Red-tailed Hawk looks as though it has been suddenly and rudely awakened. Its characteristic scream further suggests that the Red-tailed Hawk is a bird best avoided. You would think other birds would treat this large raptor with more respect, but the Red-tailed Hawk is constantly being harassed by crows, jays and blackbirds.

It isn't until this hawk is two or three years old that its tail becomes brick red. The dark head, dark brown 'belt' around its midsection and the dark leading edge to its wings are better field marks because they're seen in most Red-tails. Wherever there is an oak woodlot near open country, it's hard not to spot a Red-tail perched on a post or soaring lazily overhead.

Similar Species: Cooper's Hawk (p. 43) and Sharp-shinned Hawk are smaller, have long tails and rarely soar. Broad-winged Hawk (p. 44) has a banded tail. Northern Harrier has a white rump.

Quick I.D.: large hawk; sexes similar; brick red tail (adult only); brown head; variable brown-speckled 'belt'; light flight feathers; dark leading edge to wing lining.
Size: 20–24 in.

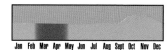

Jan Feb Mar Apr May Jun Jul Aug Sept Oct Nov Dec

American Kestrel
Falco sparverius

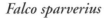

This small, noisy falcon is a common summer sight over much of the Chicago area. It has adapted well to modern rural life, and it is commonly seen perched on power lines watching for unwary grasshoppers, birds and rodents. We can also see American Kestrels as we drive off expressways on cloverleaf exits, where the small falcons hover above the long grasses in search of voles and insects.

All falcons are skilled hunters, and they have a unique, tooth-like projection on their hooked bills that can quickly crush the neck of small prey. The American Kestrel's species name, *sparverius,* is Latin for 'pertaining to sparrows,' an occasional prey item. The nests of American Kestrels are often built in abandoned woodpecker cavities. Conservationists have recently discovered that kestrels will use nest boxes when natural cavities are unavailable, which should ensure that these active predators remain common throughout the Chicago area.

Similar Species: Cooper's Hawk (p. 43) and Sharp-shinned Hawk have short, rounded wings. Merlin is larger, has a heavier-streaked breast and lacks the two facial stripes.

Quick I.D.: smaller than a jay; long, pointed wings; long tail; two vertical black stripes on face; spotted breast; hooked bill. *Male:* blue wings; russet back; colorful head. *Female:* russet back and wings. *In flight:* rapid wingbeat.
Size: 8–9 in.

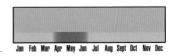

Jan Feb Mar Apr May Jun Jul Aug Sept Oct Nov Dec

Peregrine Falcon
Falco peregrinus

The Peregrine Falcon is one of the fastest animals in the world, and it can reach speeds of up to 200 m.p.h. Once a Peregrine has its prey singled out, even the fastest ducks and shorebirds have little chance of escaping this effective predator. The Peregrine Falcon plunges on its prey, punching large birds in mid-air and following them to the ground, where they are killed and eaten.

Chicago's Peregrines declined to near extinction because of pesticide residues in the environment. An active recovery plan for this endangered species has restored the population, and this magnificent bird can now be found breeding on downtown skyscrapers. These artificial cliffs seem to duplicate their natural nesting requirements, and the numerous prey species in the area also contribute to their nesting success. It is pleasantly ironic that within some of America's most developed habitats, the noble Peregrine has found sanctuary from possible extinction and can thrill desk-bound executives in their high-rise offices.

Similar Species: American Kestrel (p. 46) and Merlin are much smaller.

Jan Feb Mar Apr May Jun Jul Aug Sept Oct Nov Dec

Quick I.D.: crow-sized; sexes similar; dark blue hood extending down cheek; steel blue upper-parts; light underparts with dark speckles. *Immature:* like adult, except brown where adult is steel blue; more heavily streaked underparts. *In flight:* pointed wings; long tail.
Size: 15–20 in.

Ring-necked Pheasant
Phasianus colchicus

These spectacular birds were introduced from Asia and are now common in the Chicago region. The rooster-like *pe-cok* calls of male pheasants rise from dense, weedy fields, forest preserves and cattail marshes during winter, often surprising leisurely walkers.

During the breeding season, males collect a harem of up to five hens, which they then attempt to protect from the advances of rival males. Males are armed with a short but dangerous spur on the back of the leg, and fights between them can be fierce. Once males have mated with the harem, the females occasionally deposit their eggs into one communal nest. Whether overflowing with multiple clutches or not, pheasant nests are frequently preyed upon by Chicago's coyotes, raccoons and raptors.

Similar Species: None.

♂

Quick I.D.: hawk-sized; long, tapering tail; short, round wings. *Male:* iridescent green hood; fleshy red skin on cheeks; white 'necklace'; golden-red body plumage. *Female:* brown overall.
Size: *Male:* 31–35 in. *Female:* 21–24 in.

Jan Feb Mar Apr May Jun Jul Aug Sept Oct Nov Dec

Black-bellied Plover
Pluvialis squatarola

non-breeding

During spring and fall, Black-bellied Plovers are regularly seen darting along lakefront beaches, grassy openings and plowed fields, foraging with a robin-like run-and-stop technique. Although they dress in plain grays for much of their Chicago stay, Black-bellied Plovers can be seen in their summer tuxedo plumage in early spring and rarely in fall.

Although these plovers are most common in our area during spring and fall migration, a few birds can usually be observed poking around Chicago-area beaches during late summer and winter. Bring your binoculars with you on your next walk—if you're lucky, you might see some Black-bellied Plovers scurrying along the sand ahead of you as they pluck at the surface for food.

Similar Species: American Golden-Plover has a dark cap and lacks the white rump and black wing pits.

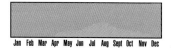

Jan Feb Mar Apr May Jun Jul Aug Sept Oct Nov Dec

Quick I.D.: larger than a robin; sexes similar; short, stout, black bill; relatively long, dark legs. *Non-breeding:* slightly streaked, gray body. *In flight:* black wing pits; white rump; white wing linings. **Size:** 11–13 in.

Killdeer
Charadrius vociferus

The Killdeer is probably the most widespread shorebird in the Chicago area. It nests on gravelly shorelines, utility rights-of-way, lawns, pastures and occasionally on gravel roofs in the city. Its name is a paraphrase of its distinctive, loud call—*kill-dee kill-dee kill-deer*—which is a harbinger of spring in our region.

The Killdeer's response to predators relies on deception and good acting skills. To divert a predator's attention away from a nest or a brood of young, an adult Killdeer (like many shorebirds) will flop around to fake an injury, usually a broken wing or leg. Once the Killdeer has the attention of the fox, crow or gull, it leads the predator away from the vulnerable nest. After it reaches a safe distance, the adult Killdeer is suddenly 'healed' and flies off, leaving the predator confused and without a meal.

Similar Species: Semipalmated Plover has only one chest band, is smaller and is found mostly on mudflats.

Quick I.D.: robin-sized; sexes similar; two black bands across breast; brown back; russet rump; long legs; white underparts.
Size: 9–11 in.

Jan Feb Mar Apr May Jun Jul Aug Sept Oct Nov Dec

Lesser Yellowlegs
Tringa flavipes

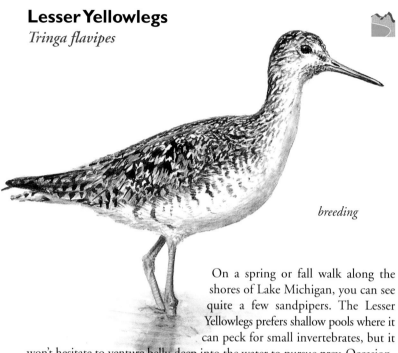

breeding

On a spring or fall walk along the shores of Lake Michigan, you can see quite a few sandpipers. The Lesser Yellowlegs prefers shallow pools where it can peck for small invertebrates, but it won't hesitate to venture belly-deep into the water to pursue prey. Occasionally, a yellowlegs can be seen hopping along on one leg, with the other one tucked up against the body feathers to reduce heat loss.

Many birders enjoy the challenge of distinguishing the Lesser Yellowlegs from the Greater Yellowlegs. The Greater, which is less common in our area (but don't let that bias your identification), has a relatively longer, heavier bill that is also slightly upturned—so slightly that you notice it one moment and not the next. Generally, the Lesser calls *tew tew*, and the Greater calls *tew tew tew*. Cocky birders will name them at a glance, but more experienced birders will tell you that many of these people are bluffing—much of the time you can only write 'unidentified yellowlegs' in your field notes.

Similar Species: Sanderling (p. 55) and Dunlin (p. 57) are much smaller and have dark legs. Greater Yellowlegs is larger and has a longer, two-toned bill generally two or three times the length of its head.

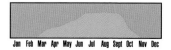

Jan Feb Mar Apr May Jun Jul Aug Sept Oct Nov Dec

Quick I.D.: robin-sized; sexes similar; long, bright yellow legs; finely streaked gray body; bill shorter than head length.
Size: 9–11 in.

Solitary Sandpiper
Tringa solitaria

True to its name, the Solitary Sandpiper is frequently seen alone or in small groups along the shores of Lake Michigan, mudflats and the edges of inland lakes and rivers. This antisocial behavior is fairly unusual among migrating shorebirds in our area, but it is this bird's habit of bobbing its body like a Latin dancer that is its most striking feature.

Solitary Sandpipers stalk shorelines, picking up aquatic invertebrates, such as waterboatmen and damselfly nymphs. Unlike most other shorebirds, these northern breeders have been known to cleverly stir the water with a foot to spook out prey.

Although Chicago-area birdwatchers will see far more of other types of shorebirds in a year, the Solitary Sandpiper is encountered frequently in our area during migration. Its voice is a high, thin *peet-wheet* or *wheet wheet wheet* during its spring passage.

Similar Species: Lesser Yellowlegs (p. 51) has bright yellow legs and no eye ring. Spotted Sandpiper (p. 53) has an incomplete eye ring, a very spotted breast and an orange, black-tipped bill.

breeding

Quick I.D.: robin-sized; sexes similar; white eye ring; short, green legs; brown-gray-spotted back; white lore; brown-gray head; neck and breast have fine white streaks; dark uppertail with black-and-white barring on the sides.
Size: 8–9 in.

Jan Feb Mar Apr May Jun Jul Aug Sept Oct Nov Dec

Spotted Sandpiper
Actitis macularia

This common shorebird of lakes and rivers has a most uncommon mating strategy. In a reversal of the gender roles of most birds, the female Spotted Sandpiper competes for males in spring. After the nest is built and the eggs are laid, the female leaves to find another mate, while the first male is left to incubate the eggs. This behavior can be repeated two or more times before the female settles down with one male to raise her last brood of chicks. Spotted Sandpipers nest in the Chicago area, and they are frequently encountered during summer and the migratory months along the undisturbed shores and rocky piers of Lake Michigan and inland wetlands and ponds.

The Spotted Sandpiper is readily identified by its arthritic-looking, stiff-winged flight low over water. Its peppy call—*eat-wheat wheat-wheat-wheat*—bursts from startled birds as they retreat from shoreline disturbances. Spotted Sandpipers constantly teeter and bob when not in flight, which makes them easy to identify.

Similar Species: Killdeer (p. 50) has dark throat bands. Solitary Sandpiper (p. 52) has an eye ring and lacks the prominent breast spots. Lesser Yellowlegs (p. 51) has longer legs.

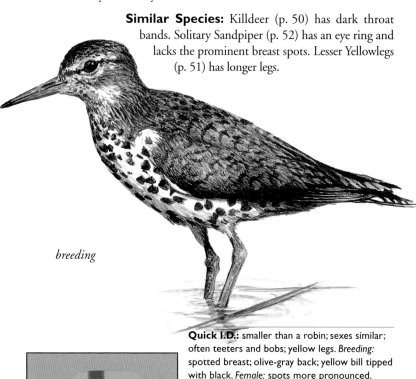

breeding

Jan Feb Mar Apr May Jun Jul Aug Sept Oct Nov Dec

Quick I.D.: smaller than a robin; sexes similar; often teeters and bobs; yellow legs. *Breeding:* spotted breast; olive-gray back; yellow bill tipped with black. *Female:* spots more pronounced.
Size: 7–8 in.

Ruddy Turnstone
Arenaria interpres

During migration, striking, harlequin-faced Ruddy Turnstones prefer sandy and pebbly beaches all along Lake Michigan's shoreline. They can be seen on jetties and beaches, where they often are seen in good numbers mixed in with other species of shorebirds. Turnstones probe in the wet sand and between small rocks for amphipods, isopods and other small invertebrates that live buried along the shoreline.

Ruddy Turnstones do much of their foraging by probing, but they have gained fame for an unusual feeding technique. As the name implies, the turnstone flips over small rocks and debris with its bill to expose hidden invertebrates. The turnstone's bill is short, stubby and slightly upturned—ideal for this foraging style.

Similar Species: Dunlin (p. 57) has a downcurved bill and lacks the bold patterning.

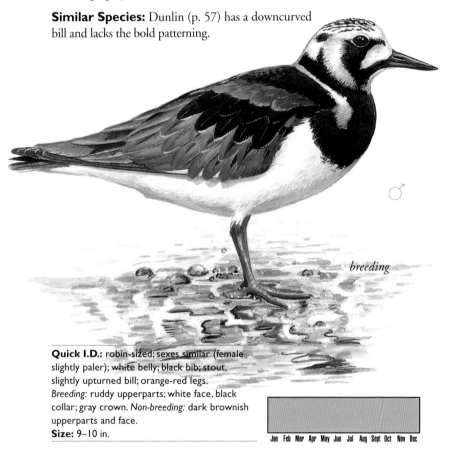

breeding

Quick I.D.: robin-sized; sexes similar (female slightly paler); white belly; black bib; stout, slightly upturned bill; orange-red legs.
Breeding: ruddy upperparts; white face, black collar; gray crown. *Non-breeding:* dark brownish upperparts and face.
Size: 9–10 in.

Jan Feb Mar Apr May Jun Jul Aug Sept Oct Nov Dec

Sanderling
Calidris alba

A spring or fall stroll along a sandy beach on Lake Michigan is often punctuated by the sight of these tiny runners, which seem to enjoy nothing more than playing in the surf. Sanderlings are characteristically seen chasing and retreating from the rolling waves, never getting caught in the charging water. Only the Sanderling commonly forages in this manner, plucking at the exposed invertebrates stirred up by the wave action. Without waves to chase along calm shorelines, Sanderlings unenthusiastically probe into wet soil in much the same fashion as many other sandpipers.

This sandpiper is one of the world's most widespread birds. It breeds across the Arctic in Alaska, Canada and Russia, and it spends winter running up and down sandy shorelines in North America, South America, Asia, Africa and Australia.

Similar Species: Least Sandpiper (p. 56) is smaller and darker. Dunlin (p. 57) is darker and has a downcurved bill.

breeding

Jan Feb Mar Apr May Jun Jul Aug Sept Oct Nov Dec

Quick I.D.: smaller than a robin; straight, black bill; dark legs. *Breeding:* rusty head and breast. *Non-breeding:* white underparts; grayish-white upperparts.
Size: 7^1/$_2$–8^1/$_2$ in.

Least Sandpiper
Calidris minutilla

non-breeding

The Least Sandpiper is the smallest of the shorebirds, but its size is not a deterrent to its migratory feats. Like most other 'peeps'—a term used to group the nearly indistinguishable *Calidris* sandpipers—the Least Sandpipers passing through Chicago migrate to the Arctic to breed.

Groups of these tiny birds can be spotted against the damp sands of beaches, mudflats and lakeshores throughout our area. Their plumage matches perfectly their preferred habitat, and it is usually their rapid movements that reveal these diminutive sprinters. Least Sandpipers tenaciously peck the moist substrate with their dexterous bills, eating mosquitoes, beach fleas, amphipods and other aquatic invertebrates.

Similar Species: Other 'peeps' tend to have dark legs and are generally larger. Pectoral Sandpiper is larger and has a well-defined pectoral border.

Quick I.D.: sparrow-sized; sexes similar; black bill; yellow legs; dark, mottled back; buff-brown breast, head and nape; light breast streaking.
Immature: like adult, but with fainter breast streaking.
Size: 5–6 in.

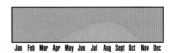

Jan Feb Mar Apr May Jun Jul Aug Sept Oct Nov Dec

Dunlin
Calidris alpina

The flocking behavior of these small, plump shorebirds is a spectacular performance. Dunlins are communal creatures, and as they pass Chicago they form a swirling cloud of individuals flying wing tip to wing tip, instantaneously changing course, hundreds behaving as if one entity. These hypnotic flights, flashing alternating shades of white and black, are occasionally seen as Dunlins migrate along Lake Michigan's shores. The flocks move both northward and southward during their trips around Lake Michigan shorelines. These tight flocks are generally more exclusive than many other shorebird troupes: few species mix with groups of Dunlins.

The Dunlin, like many other shorebirds, nests on the Arctic tundra and winters on the coasts of North America, Europe and Asia. It was originally called a 'Dunling' (meaning 'a small brown bird'), but for reasons lost to science the 'g' was later dropped.

Similar Species: Least Sandpiper (p. 56) is smaller. Sanderling (p. 55) is paler and is usually seen running in the surf.

breeding

Quick I.D.: smaller than a robin; sexes similar; slightly downcurved bill; dark legs. *Breeding:* black belly; streaked underparts; rusty back. *Non-breeding:* pale gray underparts; grayish-brown upperparts.
Size: 8–9 in.

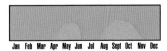

Jan Feb Mar Apr May Jun Jul Aug Sept Oct Nov Dec

Short-billed Dowitcher
Limnodromus griseus

When cool fall air descends from the north, shorebirds concentrate along muddy and flooded fields. The oncoming winter forces dowitchers and other shorebirds to retreat to the south, often packing them together in large numbers along the way. Dowitchers tend to be stockier than most of their neighboring shorebirds, and they avoid deeper water. The sewing machine–like rhythm with which dowitchers forage deeply into the mudflats is helpful for field identification.

Unfortunately, separating the two Chicago-area dowitcher species is one of the most difficult tasks any birder can attempt. Although most people are perfectly content to simply call them 'dowitchers,' some birders insist they can separate the two species by voice alone (Short-billed: *tu tu tu*; Long-billed: *keek*).

Similar Species: Common Snipe (p. 59) has longer legs, heavily barred upperparts and different foraging techniques. Long-billed Dowitcher has barring on its sides and an unmarked breast, its plumage is darker overall, and its bill is slightly longer.

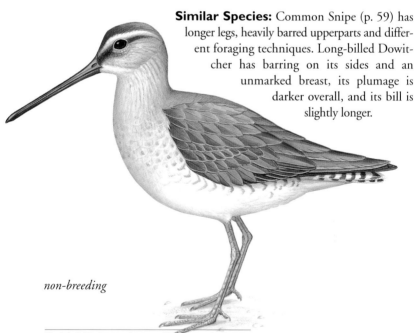

non-breeding

Quick I.D.: larger than a robin; sexes similar; very long, straight, dark bill; very stocky body; short neck. *Breeding:* reddish underparts; lightly barred flanks; dark, mottled upperparts; dark eye line; light eyebrow; dark yellow legs; white rump. *Non-breeding:* gray overall; white belly.
Size: 11–12½ in. (female larger).

Jan Feb Mar Apr May Jun Jul Aug Sept Oct Nov Dec

Common Snipe
Gallinago gallinago

These shorebirds are both secretive and well camouflaged, so few people notice them until the birds fly suddenly out of nearby grassy tussocks. As soon as snipes take to the air, they perform a series of quick zigzags, an evasive maneuver designed to confuse predators. The in-flight movements are so effective that, in times past, only the best shorebird hunters were known as 'snipers'—a term later adopted by the military. Snipes are seldom seen in large groups, nor are they normally encountered along open shorelines; their heavily streaked plumage is suited to grassy habitat.

The mystical 'winnowing' sound of courting Common Snipes is heard infrequently in the Chicago area, because their breeding habitat has largely been destroyed. However, during spring evenings at sedge meadows in Illinois Beach and Chain O'Lakes state parks, the accelerating sound, produced in flight by air passing through spread tail feathers, can thrill perceptive observers.

Similar Species: All other shorebirds are either too short of bill or not as heavily streaked.

Jan Feb Mar Apr May Jun Jul Aug Sept Oct Nov Dec

Quick I.D.: robin-sized; sexes similar; long, black-tipped bill; heavily streaked back; short neck; striped head; long legs.
Size: 10$^1/_2$–11$^1/_2$ in.

American Woodcock
Scolopax minor

For much of the year, the American Woodcock's behavior matches its cryptic and unassuming attire. This well-camouflaged bird inhabits woods and thickets—its lifestyle does little to reveal it to the outside world.

For a short month each spring, male woodcocks explode into vanity. The courtship performance begins when the male selects a clearing in the woods, where he gives a plaintive *bjeent* that inspires him into an Elvis-like boogie. The woodcock's legs are short, so he usually selects a stage that is free of thick vegetation, which would block the females' views of his swinging strut. When he has sashayed sufficiently, he takes to the air. Spiraling upward into the evening sky, he twitters increasingly toward the sky-dance climax. Upon hitting the peak of his ascent, the male woodcock relaxes and then plummets, uncontrolled, to the ground. Just before striking the ground, the woodcock pulls out of the crippled dive and alights on his dancing stage, where he resumes his breeding ballet. To attend this long-running performance, visit a moist, open woodland, such as Cuba Marsh or Illinois Beach State Park, in April or May.

Similar Species: Common Snipe (p. 59) has a striped head and back and pointed wings.

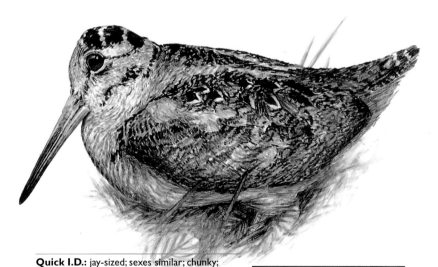

Quick I.D.: jay-sized; sexes similar; chunky; very long bill; large eyes; rusty underparts.
In flight: rounded wings.
Size: 10–12 in.

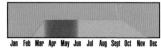

Jan Feb Mar Apr May Jun Jul Aug Sept Oct Nov Dec

Bonaparte's Gull
Larus philadelphia

The scratchy little calls of Bonaparte's Gulls accompany these migrants as they forage along Chicago's shorelines. These gulls commonly feed on the water's surface, and they can often be seen resting atop the water or circling around inland lakes and flooded fields. Bonaparte's Gulls pass through our area during the last two weeks of April and the first half of May on their way north to breed in the northern boreal forest. There they nest, in most un-gull-like fashion, in spruce trees.

After the summer breeding season, most Bonaparte's Gulls lose their distinctive black hoods, but they retain flashy white wing patches and a noticeable black spot behind the eyes. When they return to our area from September through December, they are more visible, but far less striking in appearance. This gull was named not after the famed French emperor, but after his nephew, Charles Lucien Bonaparte, who brought recognition to his family's name through the practice of ornithology.

Similar Species: Common Tern (p. 64) has a forked tail and lacks a white wing flash.

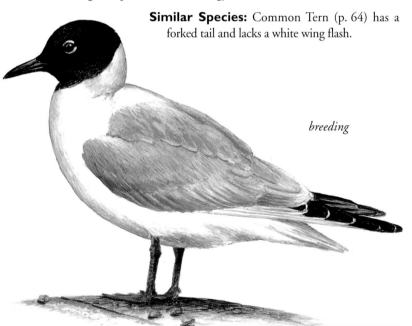

breeding

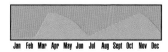

Jan Feb Mar Apr May Jun Jul Aug Sept Oct Nov Dec

Quick I.D.: small gull; sexes similar; black bill; dark eyes. *Breeding:* black hood. *Non-breeding:* white head with dark ear spot. *In flight:* wing tips have black outline; wings flash white.
Size: 12–14 in.

Ring-billed Gull
Larus delawarensis

breeding

This widespread, extremely common gull is slightly smaller than the Herring Gull and has a distinctive dark bill ring, for which it is well named. The Ring-billed Gull is frequently seen in parks and shopping center parking lots. The warm air rising from concrete and asphalt are like elevators that dozens of gulls ride simultaneously, climbing until their sleek shapes vanish into the sky.

Although these gulls seem to be regular urbanites, like so many people in Chicago, they commute daily into the city. From shoreline suburbs, gull traffic can be seen during early mornings, congested along skyways leading into town. Their daily activities involve squabbling with other greedy gulls over leftovers from fast-food restaurants and for food in open areas. When nicely fed, they might break from feeding duties by soaring high above the hectic pace of city life.

Similar Species: Herring Gull (p. 63) is larger, has pink legs and lacks the bill ring. Bonaparte's Gull (p. 61) is smaller and has a black head in spring and a white wing flash.

Quick I.D.: mid-sized gull; sexes similar; black ring near bill tip; yellow bill and legs; gray back and wing coverts; light eyes; black wing tips; small, white spots on black primaries; white underparts. *Non-breeding:* white head and nape washed with brown. *First winter:* mottled grayish brown; brown band on white tail.
Size: 18–20 in.

Jan Feb Mar Apr May Jun Jul Aug Sept Oct Nov Dec

Herring Gull
Larus argentatus

Many gulls come and go in Chicago, but the Herring Gull is a year-round resident in the Great Lakes region. This familiar bird is called a 'sea gull,' but it does not rightfully deserve that name, because the Herring Gulls seen in our area rarely venture to salt water. If this bird were to relinquish the title, however, it would likely be labeled with one even less desirable. Large flocks of Herring Gulls can be found in bays, lakes, garbage dumps, shorelines, city parks and agricultural fields, and they are mistakenly thought of as dirty birds. Herring Gulls are so widely distributed they are sure to be sighted on just about any birding trip taken along the shore of Lake Michigan.

Although often overlooked by even the most curious naturalist, the Herring Gull is an engineering marvel. Agile on land, an effortless flyer, wonderfully adaptive and with a stomach for anything digestible, Herring Gulls are perhaps the most widely distributed gull in North America.

Similar Species: Ring-billed Gull (p. 62) has yellow legs and a black-banded bill.

breeding

Quick I.D.: hawk-sized; sexes similar; white head and body; gray back; pink legs; dark wing tips; yellow eyes; red spot on lower mandible. *Immature:* variable; brown overall; all-black tail. **Size:** 24–26 in.

Common Tern
Sterna hirundo

breeding

The Common Tern generally goes unnoticed until a splash draws attention to its headfirst dives into water. Once it has firmly seized a small fish in its black-tipped bill, the tern bounces back into the air and continues its leisurely flight. Common Terns are easily observed in May, working the shores of Lake Michigan during migration. Although some remain to nest on sandbars and unvegetated islands just inland from Lake Michigan, most choose to continue north for breeding opportunities.

Although terns and gulls share many of the same physical characteristics, there are features that clearly separate the two groups. Terns seldom rest on the water, and they rarely soar in flight. They also have very short necks, pointed wings and long, forked tails, and they tend to look toward the ground during flight. Both gulls and terns tend to nest in similar regions, but this might be more convenient for the gulls, because they routinely prey on the smaller terns.

Similar Species: Caspian Tern has a large, red bill and is gull-sized. Forster's Tern has a longer, gray tail and frosted wing tips.

Quick I.D.: larger than a pigeon; sexes similar; black cap; red bill tipped with black; gray back and wings; pointed wings; white throat; light gray belly; light grayish tail. *In flight:* light grayish, forked tail; often hovers.
Size: 14–16 in.

Jan Feb Mar Apr May Jun Jul Aug Sept Oct Nov Dec

Black Tern

Chlidonias niger

Over cattail marshes, the erratic, aeronautic flight of the Black Tern is unmatched by any other bird. It dips and dives, swoops and spins in dizzying foraging flights, picking insects neatly off the water's surface and in mid-air. This tern is the master of the airways above its marshy breeding grounds, breaking only briefly to perch on a nearby post or return to its nest.

Black Terns build their nests near the cattails and vegetated islands of Lake Calumet and other marshes in our region. They nest on floating platforms or small islands. Both the male and female incubate the clutch of two to four eggs and help feed the quickly growing young.

Black Terns look like frail birds, but they are built to have dominion over the winds. When they leave our area in September, they head out to tropical coasts, to dance over foreign waters until their spring return.

Similar Species: Common Tern (p. 64) and Forster's Tern are much lighter underneath.

breeding

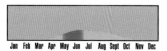

Jan Feb Mar Apr May Jun Jul Aug Sept Oct Nov Dec

Quick I.D.: robin-sized; sexes similar; gray upperparts and tail; black bill; long, pointed wings; shallowly forked tail; reddish-black legs. *Breeding:* black head, neck and underparts; white undertail coverts. *Non-breeding:* white underparts; black mark behind eye; dark gray collar on sides in front of wings.

Size: 9–11 in.

Rock Dove
Columba livia

This Eurasian native was first brought to North America in 1606 as a food source. Rock Doves were to receive the last laugh, though, because they quickly dispersed from the East Coast to colonize the entire continent. The Rock Dove (or pigeon) has taken advantage of humans for food and shelter: it lives in old buildings, on ledges and on bridges, and it feeds primarily on waste grain and human handouts. Nowhere is this bird more common than in the steep-walled canyons of Chicago's skyscrapers.

Rock Doves might appear strained when walking—their heads move back and forth with every step—but few birds are as agile in flight or as abundant in urban and industrial areas. While no other bird varies as much in coloration, all Rock Doves, whether white, red, blue or mixed-pigment, will clap their wings above and below their bodies upon take-off.

Similar Species: Mourning Dove (p. 67) is the same length as the Rock Dove, but it is slender and has a long, tapering tail and olive-brown plumage.

Quick I.D.: mid-sized pigeon; sexes similar; variable color (iridescent blue-gray, black, red or white); white rump (usually); orange feet; fleshy base to bill.
Size: 13–14 in.

Jan Feb Mar Apr May Jun Jul Aug Sept Oct Nov Dec

Mourning Dove
Zenaida macroura

Mourning Doves are frequently seen commuting to and from communal roost sites in evergreen woodlands. The Mourning Dove is a swift, direct flyer, and its wings can be heard whistling through the air. When not in flight, the peaceful *cooooo-cooooo-cooooah* call of the Mourning Dove can be heard filtering through open woodlands. These year-round residents roost inconspicuously in trees, but their soft cooing often betrays their presence.

The Mourning Dove feeds primarily on the ground, picking up grain and grit in open areas and visiting many backyard feeders in our region. It builds a flat, loose stick nest that rests flimsily on branches and trunks. Mourning Doves are attentive parents, and, like other members of the pigeon family, they feed 'milk' to their young. It isn't true milk—birds lack mammary glands—but a fluid produced by glands in the bird's crop. The chicks insert their bills down the adult's throat to eat the thick liquid.

Similar Species: Rock Dove (p. 66) has a white rump, is stockier and has a shorter tail.

Jan Feb Mar Apr May Jun Jul Aug Sept Oct Nov Dec

Quick I.D.: jay-sized; sexes similar; gray-brown plumage; long, white-trimmed, tapering tail; sleek body; dark, shiny patch below ear; orange feet; dark bill; peach-colored underparts.
Size: 11–13 in.

DOVES & PARROTS 67

Monk Parakeet
Myiopsitta monachus

Monk Parakeets occur as startling, unexpected flashes of green flying through the concrete jungle in the heart of Chicago. Such tropical sights seem oddly placed, but Monk Parakeet colonies have been thriving since the late 1970s here in our area. This introduced species, originally from South America, is quite ironically one of the few birds that residents living in the depths of Chicago's urban maze can view regularly.

Such circumstances raise questions about how these birds arrived and withstood our challenging environment. Monk Parakeets were released, or escaped as captive birds, and soon began to colonize local areas. Their nests, haystacks of sticks, are used throughout the year and shield the birds from temperatures that dip far below zero. Because there are few natural food sources, Monk Parakeets depend on the generosity of human neighbors and ornamental plants to supply them with a year-round supply of food. It is inspiring to think that these tropical flying jewels have happened to select one of America's most altered environments to bring to us a sense of wildness.

Similar Species: None.

Quick I.D.: larger than a jay; sexes similar; green upperparts, wings and tail; heavy, yellow, hooked bill; grayish face and throat; bluish flight feathers; yellow-green belly.
Size: 11 1/2 in.

Jan Feb Mar Apr May Jun Jul Aug Sept Oct Nov Dec

Eastern Screech-Owl
Otus asio

Despite its small size, the Eastern Screech-Owl is an adaptable hunter. It has a varied diet that ranges from insects, earthworms and fish to birds larger than itself. Silent and reclusive by day, screech-owls hunt at night.

Some owls' senses are refined for darkness and their bodies for silence: their large, forward-facing eyes have many times more light-gathering sensors than do ours, and the wings of nocturnal owls are edged with soft, frayed feathers for silent flight. Their ears, located on the sides of their heads, are asymmetrical (one is higher than the other), which enables these birds to track sounds more easily. Given these adaptations, it is no surprise that owls have successfully invaded nearly all of the world's major ecosystems.

gray phase

A birder with a keen ear, while strolling along the wooded paths of ravines, river valleys and hardwood forests during early spring evenings, will hear the distinctive whistled voice of the Eastern Screech-Owl. The call's rhythm has often been compared to that of a bouncing ball coming to rest.

Similar Species: Northern Saw-whet Owl has a dark facial disc and no ear tufts, and its call does not increase in pace.

Jan Feb Mar Apr May Jun Jul Aug Sept Oct Nov Dec

Quick I.D.: robin-sized; sexes similar; short, widely spaced ear tufts; heavy vertical streaking and bars on chest; yellow eyes; dark bill; two color phases (gray, which is more common, and red).
Size: 8–9 in. (female slightly larger).

Great Horned Owl
Bubo virginianus

The Great Horned Owl is the most widely distributed owl in North America, and it is among the most formidable of predators. It uses specialized hearing, powerful talons and human-sized eyes during nocturnal hunts for mice, rabbits, quails, amphibians and occasionally fish. It has a poorly developed sense of smell, however, which is why it can prey on skunks—worn-out and discarded Great Horned Owl feathers are often identifiable by a simple sniff.

The deep, resonant hooting of the Great Horned Owl is easily imitated, often leading to interesting exchanges between bird and birder. The call's deep tone is not as distinctive as its pace, which closely follows the rhythm of *Eat my food, I'll-eat yooou*. The calls and the bird's distinctive silhouette can even be encountered at night in Chicago-area subdivisions.

Similar Species: Eastern Screech-Owl (p. 69) is much smaller and has vertical breast streaking. Long-eared Owl has a slimmer body and vertical streaks on its chest, and its ear tufts are very close together.

Quick I.D.: hawk-sized; sexes similar; large, widely spaced ear tufts; fine, horizontal chest bars; dark brown plumage; white throat.
Size: 18–25 in.

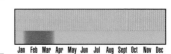

Jan Feb Mar Apr May Jun Jul Aug Sept Oct Nov Dec

Common Nighthawk
Cordeiles minor

The Common Nighthawk, which is unrelated to true hawks, has a Dr. Jekyll and Mr. Hyde split personality. Mild-mannered by day, it rests on the ground or on a horizontal tree branch, its color and shape blending perfectly into the texture of the bark. At dusk, the Common Nighthawk takes on a new form as a dazzling and erratic flyer, catching insects in flight.

To many people, the sound of the nighthawk is the sound of summer evenings, when the birds leave their gravel rooftop nests to court over the city. The nighthawks repeatedly call out with a loud, nasal *peeent* as they circle high overhead, then they dive suddenly toward the ground and create a hollow *vroom* sound by thrusting their wings forward at the last possible moment, pulling out of the dive.

Similar Species: Whip-poor-will (p. 72) and Chuck-will's-widow have rounded wings and tails.

Quick I.D.: robin-sized; sexes similar; cryptic, light to dark brown plumage. *Male:* white throat. *Female:* buff throat. *In flight:* shallowly forked tail; long, pointed wings; white wrist bands; flight is erratic.
Size: 9–10 in.

Whip-poor-will
Caprimulgus vociferus

Although heard far more often than it is seen, the Whip-poor-will makes identification easy for novice birdwatchers because this nighttime hunter fills evenings with its own name. The distinctive *whip-poor-will* is chanted persistently at the rate of about once per second. At prime Whip-poor-will sites, such as Indiana Dunes and Illinois Beach state parks, these birds sing continuously from dusk to dawn.

The Whip-poor-will arrives in the Chicago area by the end of April and soon finds an open woodland in which to nest. No nest is constructed; rather, the eggs are simply laid on bare ground. These well-camouflaged birds also choose to roost during the day on bare ground, and at dusk they can occasionally be seen resting on or alongside roadsides.

The Iroquois were obviously respectful of these birds, because, according to legend, the flowers of wild moccasin plants were thought to be the shoes of Whip-poor-wills.

Similar Species: Common Nighthawk (p. 71) has pointed wings, a notched tail and white wrist bands.

Quick I.D.: robin-sized; gray-brown plumage; wings and tail rounded; black throat; light outer tail feathers; light 'necklace'. *Male:* white outer tail feathers and 'necklace'. *Female:* buff 'necklace' and outer tail feathers.
Size: 9–10 in.

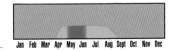

Jan Feb Mar Apr May Jun Jul Aug Sept Oct Nov Dec

Belted Kingfisher

Ceryle alcyon

Where open water is found in the Chicago area, Belted Kingfishers can be encountered every day of the year, crashing into calm waters in search of fish. A dead branch extending over water will often serve as a perch from which to survey the fish below, which they catch with precise headfirst dives. Although there are many species of kingfisher in the world, the Belted Kingfisher is the only member of its family across most of the United States.

The Belted Kingfisher builds its nest near the end of a long tunnel excavated a few feet into sandy or dirt banks. A rattling call, like a teacup shaking on a saucer, is likely more useful in finding these birds than their trademark plumage. With most birds, the males are more colorful, but female kingfishers are distinguished from males by the presence of a second, rust-colored band across the belly.

Similar Species: None.

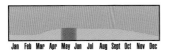

Jan Feb Mar Apr May Jun Jul Aug Sept Oct Nov Dec

Quick I.D.: pigeon-sized; blue-gray back, wings and head; shaggy crest; heavy bill. *Male:* single, blue chest band. *Female:* blue chest band; rust-colored 'belt'.
Size: 12–14 in.

Red-headed Woodpecker
Melanerpes erythrocephalus

'His tri-coloured plumage, so striking. ... A gay and frolicsome disposition, diving and vociferating around the high dead limbs of some large tree, amusing the passenger with their gambols.'

—Alexander Wilson

When Wilson landed in North America, the Scotsman, with little money and few skills, did not know what he'd do in the New World. Like a revelation, a Red-headed Woodpecker was one of the first birds to greet the immigrant. Never had Wilson seen such beauty, and the bird inspired the future 'father of American ornithology' to devote his life to birds. With no formal ornithological background, he went on to discover and describe dozens of North American species. Although the Red-headed Woodpecker's plumage might not drive everyone to great scientific achievements, look for these wondrous beauties at Illinois Beach or Indiana Dunes state parks and become impassioned by their beauty.

Similar Species: Red-bellied Woodpecker (p. 75) has a gray cheek and black-and-white zebra stripes on its back.

Quick I.D.: robin-sized; sexes similar; stunning red head and throat; black back and tail; white rump, inner wing patches and belly.
Immature: brownish head; bars on white wing patches, dirty white underparts.
Size: 8–9 in.

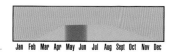

Jan Feb Mar Apr May Jun Jul Aug Sept Oct Nov Dec

Red-bellied Woodpecker
Melanerpes carolinus

An unexpected barking *churr* in mixed woodlands anywhere in our area is often the first clue that the oddly named Red-bellied Woodpecker is about. A fairly common resident in our area, this woodpecker mysteriously acquired a name that reflects a very subtle field mark. Since the 'Red-headed' name is granted to a more deserving woodpecker, perhaps the most suitable name would have been the 'Zebra-backed Woodpecker.'

♂

♀

Regardless of its unusual name, this woodpecker has recently enjoyed a slight increase in population in our area. Although the Red-bellied Woodpecker is continually threatened by bullying European Starlings, the regeneration of Midwestern forests has encouraged the dispersal of these birds. Interestingly, birdfeeders have also played a role in their recent successes by increasing their survival through our winters. Many Chicago birdwatchers fondly remember the chilly winter day when this striking bird first visited their suet or sunflower seed feeder. Although the seed source might be completely reliable throughout the cold months, Red-bellied Woodpeckers take no chances, and hoard the food, filling tree cavities, gaps in shingles and other small spaces with insurance seeds.

Similar Species: Red-headed Woodpecker (p. 74) has a solid red head and a solid black upper back. Northern Flicker (p. 78) has black spotting on its underparts, yellow wing and tail linings and lacks the black-and-white barring on the back.

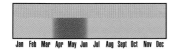

Jan Feb Mar Apr May Jun Jul Aug Sept Oct Nov Dec

Quick I.D.: robin-sized; black-and-white barring on back; red crown and nape; plain gray face and underparts; very faint red belly; white rump. *Male:* red forehead. *Female:* gray forehead. **Size:** 9 in.

Northern Flicker
Colaptes auratus

Walkers strolling through Lincoln Park might be surprised by a woodpecker flushing from the ground before them. As the Northern Flicker beats a hasty retreat, it reveals an unmistakable white rump and yellow wing linings. It is the least arboreal of our woodpeckers, and it spends more time feeding on the ground than other woodpeckers. Often it is only when the Northern Flicker is around its nest cavity in a tree that it truly behaves like other woodpeckers: clinging, rattling and drumming.

The Northern Flicker can easily be seen all year in our area, and it visits backyard feeders particularly during winter. The Northern Flicker (and other birds) squash ants and then preen themselves with the remains. Ants contain concentrations of formic acid, which is believed to kill small parasites living on the flicker's skin and in its feathers.

Similar Species: Red-bellied Woodpecker (p. 75) has a red crown and black-and-white stripes on its back.

Quick I.D.: jay-sized; brown-barred back; spotted underparts; black bib; white rump; long bill; yellow wing and tail feathers; gray crown; red nape. *Male:* black mustache. *Female:* no mustache.
Size: 11–14 in.

Jan Feb Mar Apr May Jun Jul Aug Sept Oct Nov Dec

Ruby-throated Hummingbird
Archilochus colubris

Everyone knows and loves the tiny hummingbird that buzzes into flowerbeds and visits special feeders throughout summer. These miniature birds span the ecological gap between birds and insects, feeding on the energy-rich nectar that flower blooms provide in exchange for the feeder's pollinating assistance. Perhaps it is the bird's remarkable size, or its intimate association with flowers, that make smiles appear whenever these birds are discussed.

The Ruby-throated Hummingbird is the only bird of its kind to uncommonly breed in the Chicago area. As such, it is interesting to look at this species and admire one of nature's engineering marvels. Weighing about the same as a quarter, hummingbirds are capable of speeds of up to 60 m.p.h.! In straight-ahead flight they beat their wings up to 80 times per second (slightly less if hovering or reversing), and in migration they cross the Gulf of Mexico, an incredible non-stop journey of over 620 miles. Although impressive, the astonishing intricacy and sophistication possessed by the Ruby-throated Hummingbird may be overshadowed by the inescapable joy carried by this bird upon its tiny wings.

Similar Species: None.

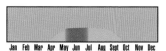

Jan Feb Mar Apr May Jun Jul Aug Sept Oct Nov Dec

Quick I.D.: our smallest bird; iridescent green back, long, thin, dark bill; light underparts; dark tail. *Male:* iridescent red throat. *Female* and *Immature:* fine streaking on throat.
Size: 3³/₄ in.

Eastern Wood-Pewee
Contopus virens

The plaintive, whistled *pee-a-wee* of
the Eastern Wood-Pewee echoes sadly
through most woodlands in our area.
These mouse-colored summer residents are difficult to
sight until they loop out after a passing insect. A classic flycatcher, Eastern Wood-Pewees faithfully return to their preferred perch, at the mid-level in the forest, following each short
foraging flight.

The nest of the Eastern Wood-Pewee resembles nothing more than a
knot on a small limb, well camouflaged by both shape and color. The outer
walls of the structure are wallpapered with lichens, while the nest itself seems
too small for the bird sitting upon it. In addition to its concealing master-
piece, this small flycatcher vigorously defends its nest site against all intruders
who dare approach.

Similar Species: Willow Flycatcher (p. 81) has an eye ring and sings an
abrupt *fitz-bew* song. Acadian Flycatcher has a bold eye ring and a yellow
wash on its belly.

Quick I.D.: sparrow-sized; sexes similar; olive-
gray body; dark tail and wings; two faint wing
bars; no eye ring; dark upper mandible; pale
orange lower mandible.
Size: 6–6¹/₂ in.

Willow Flycatcher
Empidonax traillii

Southern spring winds carry the first Willow Flycatchers into Illinois forests in mid- to late May. The day of their arrival is often easily recognized, because these small birds punctuate their presence with their simple and sneezy *fitz-bew* song. From swaying shrubby perches, Willow Flycatchers sing and survey their chosen territories.

The Willow Flycatcher is one of the boldest and most pugnacious songbirds in the open second-growth shrub forests of Illinois. During the nesting season, it is noisy and aggressive, driving away all avian intruders and fighting furiously with rival males. The confusing collection of empidonax flycatchers are the 'lords of the mosquitoes,' but the curse of the birdwatcher. The Willow, Least, Acadian and Alder flycatchers all pass through our area each year, and they are virtually indistinguishable in the field except by voice. Their confusing plumage, however, should not deter novice birders from the pleasantness of these small birds.

Similar Species: Eastern Wood-Pewee (p. 80) sings *pee-a-wee*. All other empidonax flycatchers have more pronounced eye rings and characteristic vocalizations: Acadian Flycatcher sings *peet seet*; Least Flycatcher sings *che bek*; Alder Flycatcher sings *fee-bee-o*.

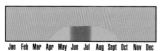

Jan Feb Mar Apr May Jun Jul Aug Sept Oct Nov Dec

Quick I.D.: sparrow-sized; sexes similar; olive-brown upperparts; no eye ring; two white wing bars; long, narrow, dark tail; dark bill; light throat.
Size: 5–6 in.

Great Crested Flycatcher
Myiarchus crinitus

The Great Crested Flycatcher is most unusual in its selection of decor for its nest cavity: it occasionally lays a shed snakeskin as a door mat. This uncommon but noteworthy practice can identify the nest of this flycatcher, the only member of its family in Chicago to nest in a cavity. The objective of the Great Crested Flycatcher's infrequently seen nest decoration is not known, and these versatile birds have occasionally substituted plastic wrap for reptilian skin.

The Great Crested Flycatcher's name is somewhat misleading—this bird's crest can only truthfully be considered 'great' when compared to those of other flycatchers. Nevertheless, an objective opinion of this bird's name and behavior can be made after pleasant encounters along Chicago's lakefront parks or in woods along the Des Plaines River. Listen for it singing its distinctive *creep creep*.

Similar Species: Eastern Wood-Pewee (p. 80), Eastern Phoebe and other flycatchers are smaller and lack the lemon yellow belly and chestnut tail.

Quick I.D.: smaller than a robin; sexes similar; yellow belly; gray throat and head; dark olive-brown back and wings; chestnut tail lining; rufous wing linings; erect crest.
Size: 7–8 in.

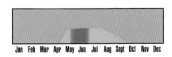

Jan Feb Mar Apr May Jun Jul Aug Sept Oct Nov Dec

Eastern Kingbird
Tyrannus tyrannus

When one thinks of a tyrant, the image of a large, carnivorous dinosaur or a menacing ruler is much more likely to come to mind than that of a little bird. While the Eastern Kingbird may not initially seem to be as imposing as other known tyrants, this flycatcher certainly lives up to its scientific name, *Tyrannus tyrannus*. The Eastern Kingbird is pugnacious—it will fearlessly attack crows, hawks, other large birds and even humans who pass through its territory. The intruders are often vigorously pursued, pecked and plucked for some distance until the kingbird is satisfied that there is no further threat.

The courtship flight of the Eastern Kingbird, which can be seen occasionally in our area, is characterized by short, quivering wingbeats. It is a touching display, even for this little tyrant. The nest site is typically close to water, where the bird's next meal is only a sudden foraging flight away.

Similar Species: Tree Swallow (p. 86) and all other flycatchers lack the white terminal tail band and are not black and white.

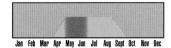

Jan Feb Mar Apr May Jun Jul Aug Sept Oct Nov Dec

Quick I.D.: smaller than a robin; sexes similar; black head, back, wings and tail; white underparts; white terminal tail band; orange-red crown (rarely seen).
Size: 9 in.

Chimney Swift
Chaetura pelagica

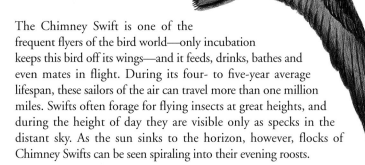

The Chimney Swift is one of the frequent flyers of the bird world—only incubation keeps this bird off its wings—and it feeds, drinks, bathes and even mates in flight. During its four- to five-year average lifespan, these sailors of the air can travel more than one million miles. Swifts often forage for flying insects at great heights, and during the height of day they are visible only as specks in the distant sky. As the sun sinks to the horizon, however, flocks of Chimney Swifts can be seen spiraling into their evening roosts.

Swifts are shaped much like swallows—long, tapering wings, a small bill, a wide gape and a long, sleek body—but they share no close relationship. The wingbeat of swifts looks uncomfortable, but it doesn't hamper the graceful flight of these aerial masters, which cast a distinct boomerang silhouette when they glide. Swifts, when not in flight, use their small but strong claws to cling precariously to vertical surfaces. Because many old, hollow hardwood trees have been removed from our area since colonization, Chimney Swifts have adopted human structures, such as inactive chimneys, as common nesting sites.

Similar Species: All swallows have a smooth, direct flight style and broader wings.

Quick I.D.: smaller than a sparrow; sexes similar; boomerang flight profile; brown overall; slim.
Size: 5¹/₂ in.

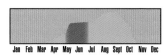

Jan Feb Mar Apr May Jun Jul Aug Sept Oct Nov Dec

Purple Martin
Progne subis

Late summer is a very busy time around a Purple Martin complex. Adults spiral around the large, communal next box, coming and going from foraging forays. The year's young perch at the opening of their apartment cavity, impatiently waiting for their parents to return with a mouthful of flying insects. A patient observer watching the colonies at the Chicago Botanic Garden will notice how orderly the apparent confusion is to the martin, and how efficiently the crowded complex is negotiated.

These fascinating experiences are rewards to residents who erect Purple Martin complexes, which should be high on a pole in the middle of a large, open area often near a large waterbody. The complex should be cleaned and plugged up once the birds have left, until they return in spring. House Sparrows and European Starlings will overthrow the preferred tenant if given a chance.

Similar Species: Barn Swallow (p. 88) has a deeply forked tail. Tree Swallow (p. 86) has a white belly. European Starling (p. 117) has a long bill and a short tail.

Quick I.D.: smaller than a robin; pointed wings; forked tail; small bill. *Male:* deep, glossy blue plumage. *Female* and *Immature:* gray underparts; duller backs.
Size: 7–8 in.

Jan Feb Mar Apr May Jun Jul Aug Sept Oct Nov Dec

Tree Swallow
Tachycineta bicolor

Depending on food availability, Tree Swallows forage over great distances, darting above open fields and wetlands as they catch flying insects in their bills. These bicolored birds occasionally swoop down to the water's surface for a quick drink and bath. In bad weather, Tree Swallows might fly up to five miles to distant marshes or lakes to find flying insects.

The Tree Swallow is among the first migrants to arrive in the Chicago area, often beating the onset of spring weather. It returns to our freshwater marshes by late March to begin its reproductive cycle. It nests in abandoned woodpecker cavities and in nest boxes intended primarily for bluebirds. The cavity is lined with weeds, grasses and long feathers. When the parents leave the nest for long periods of time, they cover the eggs with feathers. The females lay and incubate four to six eggs for up to 16 days. Once the birds hatch, the young leave the cavity within three weeks to begin their aerial lives.

Similar Species: Chimney Swift (p. 84) has slimmer wings and a darker belly. Bank Swallow (p. 87) and Northern Rough-winged Swallow both lack the blue upperparts.

Quick I.D.: sparrow-sized; sexes similar; iridescent blue plumage; white underparts; dark rump; small bill and feet. *In flight:* long, pointed wings; shallowly forked tail.
Size: 5–6 in.

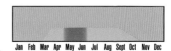

Jan Feb Mar Apr May Jun Jul Aug Sept Oct Nov Dec

Bank Swallow
Riparia riparia

Bank Swallows cruise over wetlands, fields and meadows at low altitudes, gracefully catching flying insects in flight. They often catch transforming insects just as they are emerging from the water to enter their adult stage.

Bank Swallows begin nesting in April. As their name suggests, they choose dirt banks, such as those found in gravel pits and at Waukegan Beach, in which to build their nest cavity. These small birds diligently excavate the burrow, first with their small bill and later with their feet. Incredibly, Bank Swallows have been known to kick and scratch out a burrow five feet long, but the typical length is two to three feet. An active Bank Swallow colony is difficult to approach undetected, because the frightened birds launch themselves from their burrows and circle overhead until the threat passes.

Similar Species: Tree Swallow (p. 86) has blue upperparts. Northern Rough-winged Swallow lacks the dark chest band.

Jan Feb Mar Apr May Jun Jul Aug Sept Oct Nov Dec

Quick I.D.: sparrow-sized; sexes similar; brown upperparts; light underparts; dark band on chest; long, pointed wings; small bill; dark cheek; dark rump; small legs.
Size: 5–6 in.

Barn Swallow
Hirundo rustica

The graceful flight of the Barn Swallow is a common summer sight. It often forages at low altitudes, so its deeply forked tail is easily observed. The Barn Swallow is actually the only swallow in Chicago to have a 'swallow-tail.' The name 'swallow' originated in Europe, where the Barn Swallow is also common, and where it is simply called the Swallow.

The Barn Swallow builds its cup-shaped mud nests in the eaves of barns, bridges and picnic shelters, or in any other structure that provides protection from the rain. Because the Barn Swallow is often closely associated with human structures, it is not uncommon for a nervous parent bird to dive repeatedly at human 'intruders,' encouraging them to retreat.

Similar Species: Purple Martin (p. 85) has a shorter tail and lacks the russet throat and forehead.

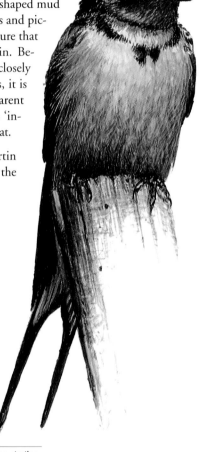

Quick I.D.: larger than a sparrow; sexes similar, but female is a bit duller; deeply forked tail; glossy blue back, wings and tail; chestnut underparts; russet throat and forehead.
Size: 6–8 in.

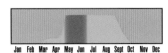

Jan Feb Mar Apr May Jun Jul Aug Sept Oct Nov Dec

Blue Jay

Cyanocitta cristata

The Blue Jay is one of our region's most identifiable birds. With its loud *jay-jay-jay* call, blue-and-white plumage and large crest, it is familiar to anyone with sunflower seeds or peanuts at their birdfeeder. Blue Jays are intelligent, aggressive and adaptable birds that don't hesitate to drive smaller birds, squirrels or even cats away when they feel threatened. Although present year-round, Blue Jays seem more numerous and noticeable throughout our winter months.

The Blue Jay represents all the admirable virtues and aggressive qualities of the corvid family. While it is beautiful, resourceful and vocally diverse, the Blue Jay can be one of the most annoying and mischievous birds, and no predator is too formidable for this bird to harass. With noisy calls, Blue Jays wake up neighborhoods and forests where they are the self-appointed guardians, but this colorful bird's extroverted character and boldness outweigh its occasional briefly annoying behavior.

Similar Species: None.

Jan Feb Mar Apr May Jun Jul Aug Sept Oct Nov Dec

Quick I.D.: larger than a robin; sexes similar; blue crest, back, wings and tail; black 'necklace'; white wing bars; light belly.
Size: 11–12 in.

American Crow

Corvus brachyrhynchos

The American Crow calls with a classic, long, descending *caaaw*. In late summer and fall, when their reproductive duties are completed, crows group together to roost in flocks, known as a 'murders.' The crow population has exploded in our area in recent years, and large flocks can be seen almost anywhere in and around Chicago.

This large, black bird's intelligence has led it into many confrontations with humans, from which it often emerges the victor. Scientific studies have shown that crows are capable of solving simple problems, which comes as no surprise to anyone who has watched crows snip open garbage bags with scissors-like precision.

Similar Species: None.

Quick I.D.: small gull–sized; sexes similar; all black; fan-shaped tail; slim overall.
Size: 18–20 in.

Jan Feb Mar Apr May Jun Jul Aug Sept Oct Nov Dec

Black-capped Chickadee
Poecile atricapillus

The Black-capped Chickadee is one of the most pleasant birds in urban and forested areas, often seeming to greet walkers along trails. It is a common sight in Chicago and can be found in every wooded area in parks and in most landscaped backyards. Throughout most of the year, chickadees move about in loose flocks, investigating nooks and crannies for food and uttering their delicate *chick-a-dee-dee-dee* calls.

During spring, Black-capped Chickadees seem strangely absent from city parks and wooded ravines, because they remain inconspicuous while nesting. Once the first fall chill arrives, the woods are once again vibrant with their busy activities.

Similar Species: White-breasted Nuthatch (p. 92) lacks a black chin and has a short tail and red undertail coverts. Tufted Titmouse lacks a black cap and bib. Blackpoll Warbler is a migrant that has orange legs and streaked underparts.

Jan Feb Mar Apr May Jun Jul Aug Sept Oct Nov Dec

Quick I.D.: smaller than a sparrow; sexes similar; black cap and bib; white cheek; grayish back, wings and tail; light underparts.
Size: 5–6 in.

White-breasted Nuthatch
Sitta carolinensis

To the novice birdwatcher, seeing a White-breasted Nuthatch call repeatedly while clinging to the underside of a branch is an odd sight. To nuthatches, however, this gravity-defying act is as natural as flight is to other birds. A nuthatch will frequently pause in mid-descent, arch its head out at right angles to the trunk and give its distinctive and often repeated *yarnk-yarnk-yarnk* call. It makes its seemingly dangerous headfirst hops seem routine.

White-breasted Nuthatches frequently visit backyard feeders. Nuthatches seem less at home on the level platform feeders, where they cast aside their tree-trunk talent for a cautious meal of sunflower seeds.

Similar Species: Black-capped Chickadee (p. 91) has a black bib and a longer tail. Red-breasted Nuthatch has a red breast and a black eye line.

♂

Quick I.D.: sparrow-sized. *Male:* black cap; white cheek and breast; steel blue back, wings and tail; straight bill; short tail; russet undertail coverts. *Female:* similar but with a grayish cap.
Size: 6 in.

Jan Feb Mar Apr May Jun Jul Aug Sept Oct Nov Dec

House Wren
Troglodytes aedon

This common bird of backyards, city parks and woodlands sings as though its lungs were bottomless. The sweet, warbling song of the House Wren is distinguished by its melodious tone and its uninterrupted endurance. Although the House Wren is far smaller than a sparrow, it offers an unending song in one breath.

Like all wrens, the House Wren frequently carries its short tail cocked straight up. This bird is often observed from May to September skulking beneath the dense understory. House Wrens seem particularly fond of shrubby bottom woods, where they nest in tree cavities or near bluebird boxes. As spring arrives, the House Wren treats Chicago neighborhoods to a few weeks of wonderful warbles, and then it channels its energy to the task of reproduction.

Similar Species: Winter Wren has cinnamon plumage and its tail is shorter than its legs. Carolina Wren has white eyebrows.

Jan Feb Mar Apr May Jun Jul Aug Sept Oct Nov Dec

Quick I.D.: smaller than a sparrow; sexes similar; brown overall; tail is often cocked up; bill is slightly downcurved; tail is as long as legs. **Size:** 5 in.

Marsh Wren
Cistothorus palustris

This energetic little bird usually lives in cattail marshes, where its distinctive voice is one of the characteristic sounds of our freshwater wetlands. In early spring, Illinois Beach State Park rings with the dynamic call of this reclusive bird. The song has the repetitive quality of an old sewing machine. Once you learn the rhythm, you will hear it on every spring visit to a freshwater wetland.

A typical sighting of a Marsh Wren is spotting a brown blur moving noisily about within cattails. Although the wren might be less than three yards from the observer, its cryptic habits and appearance are effective camouflage. Patient observers might be rewarded with a brief glimpse of a Marsh Wren perching high atop a cattail reed as it quickly evaluates its territory.

Similar Species: House Wren (p. 93) has an unstreaked back and generally avoid wetlands.

Quick I.D.: smaller than a sparrow; sexes similar; brown overall; white streaking on back; white eye line; light throat and breast; cocked-up tail.
Size: 4–5^1/$_2$ in.

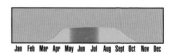

| Jan | Feb | Mar | Apr | May | Jun | Jul | Aug | Sept | Oct | Nov | Dec |

Golden-crowned Kinglet
Regulus satrapa

The high-pitched, tinkling voice of the Golden-crowned Kinglet is as familiar as the sweet smell of pine and fir in coniferous forests. Although not immediately obvious to the uninformed passerby, a birdwatcher with a keen ear, patience and the willingness to draw down this smallest of North American songbirds with squeaks and pishes will encounter kinglets on many outdoor trips. During late fall, early winter and early spring, tall conifers in Chicago's parks and older communities come alive with the sound of the Golden-crowned Kinglet's faint, high-pitched, accelerating *tsee-tsee-tsee-tsee, why do you shilly-shally?*

As these tiny birds descend in loose flocks around a curious onlooker, their indistinct plumage and voice offer little excitement. It is when the flock circles nearby, using the branches as swings and trapezes, flashing their regal crowns, that the magic of the kinglet emerges.

Similar Species: Ruby-crowned Kinglet (p. 96) lacks the black outline to the crown.

Jan Feb Mar Apr May Jun Jul Aug Sept Oct Nov Dec

Quick I.D.: smaller than a sparrow; plump; dark olive; white wing bars; dark tail and wings; white eyebrows. *Male:* fiery orange crown bordered by yellow and black. *Female:* lemon yellow crown bordered by black.
Size: 4 in.

Ruby-crowned Kinglet

Regulus calendula

These kinglets are visitors to Chicago parks and backyards, especially among coniferous trees. Kinglets always appear nervous, with their tails and wings flicking continuously as they hop from branch to branch in search of grubs and insect eggs.

The Ruby-crowned Kinglet is similar to the Golden-crowned Kinglet in size, habits and coloration, but it has a hidden ruby crown. 'Rubies' are heard more often then they are seen, and they produce an amazing amount of noise for birds of their size. Their distinctive song starts like a motor chugging to life, and then the kinglets fire off a series of loud, rising *chewy-chewy-chewy-chewys*. These final excitable phrases are often the only recognizable part of the song.

Similar Species: Golden-crowned Kinglet (p. 95) has a black outline to the crown.

Quick I.D.: smaller than a sparrow; plump; dark olive; white wing bars; dark tail and wings; incomplete eye ring. *Male:* red crown (infrequently seen). *Female:* no red crown.
Size: 4 in.

Blue-gray Gnatcatcher
Polioptila caerulea

♂

breeding

The Blue-gray Gnatcatcher's tail, which is almost as long as its body, constantly waves lazily from side to side during the bird's treetop foraging. Even in soft winds, the gnatcatcher's tail catches the breeze and seems to nearly topple the small bird. Gnatcatchers are energetic birds that flit out to catch flying insects or bounce along branches looking for prey. Although they probably eat gnats, these insects do not represent a substantial portion of their diet.

Blue-gray Gnatcatchers build their small nests at mid-height in a deciduous tree, often in riparian river courses. Both sexes build the structure and cleverly conceal its identity by plastering the outside with lichens and spider silk. Females lay four or five small eggs, and often attempt a second brood during July. These small birds are expanding their range and becoming increasingly common throughout our area, creating a wondrous diversion to attentive eyes that drift to our treetops.

Similar Species: Ruby-crowned Kinglet (p. 96) and Golden-crowned Kinglet (p. 95) are olive-green overall, with short tails and wing bars. Gray Catbird (p. 118) is much larger and has russet undertail coverts.

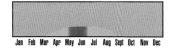

Jan Feb Mar Apr May Jun Jul Aug Sept Oct Nov Dec

Quick I.D.: smaller than a sparrow; long tail; white eye ring; pale gray underparts; no wing bars; tail is black above with white outer tail feathers. *Breeding male:* dark blue-gray upperparts; black-bordered crown. *Female:* light gray upperparts.
Size: 4¹/₂–5 in.

Eastern Bluebird
Sialia sialis

Dressed with the colors of the cool sky on its back and the warm setting sun on its chest, the male Eastern Bluebird looks like a piece of pure sky come to life. To fully appreciate this specialty, try to spot a male as he sets up his territory on a crisp, early spring morning in open country, such as at Illinois Beach State Park or Ryerson Woods.

The Eastern Bluebird lost many of its natural nesting sites in vacant cavities to House Sparrows and European Starlings and to the removal of dead trees from much of our area. Concerned residents rallied for this bird, however, and put up hundreds of nesting boxes to compensate for the losses. The Eastern Bluebird population has slowly increased as a result, and the vigilant residents have been rewarded with the sight of the bird's beautiful plumage in the Midwest's landscape.

Similar Species: American Robin (p. 101) has a dark back and lacks any blue. Male Indigo Bunting (p. 141) lacks the red breast and has a conical bill.

Quick I.D.: smaller than a robin. *Male:* sky blue back; rusty throat and breast; white undertail coverts; thin bill. *Female:* less intense blue.
Size: 6–7 in.

Jan Feb Mar Apr May Jun Jul Aug Sept Oct Nov Dec

Veery
Catharus fuscescens

Like a tumbling waterfall, the Veery's voice descends with a liquid ripple. This bird, like all other thrushes, is a master of melodies and offers its unequaled songs to forests gradually darkening with the setting sun. The Veery is one of the last singers in the evening, and if you turn your ear to woodlands along the Des Plaines River or at Volo Bog during the last weeks of May, you'll have an audio treat.

The Veery is perhaps the most terrestrial of Chicago's thrushes; it frequently nests on the ground. In characteristic thrush style, the Veery searches for grubs and caterpillars by shuffling through loose leaf litter. When an invertebrate delicacy is found, it is swallowed quickly, and the ever-vigilant Veery cautiously looks about before renewing the hunt.

Similar Species: Wood (p. 100), Hermit and Swainson's thrushes are more boldly patterned on the breast, and each has a characteristic song.

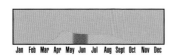

Jan Feb Mar Apr May Jun Jul Aug Sept Oct Nov Dec

Quick I.D.: smaller than a robin; sexes similar; reddish-brown head, back, rump and tail; faint spotting on throat; no conspicuous eye ring.
Size: 7–8 in.

Wood Thrush
Hylocichla mustelina

The Wood Thrush's musical warble—*Will you live with me? Way up high in a tree, I'll come right down and ... seeee*—has faded from many Illinois woodlands. The Wood Thrush was once the voice of our hardwood forests, but this species has declined because of forest fragmentation. Broken forests invite common predators, such as the skunk, fox, crow and jay, which traditionally had no access to Wood Thrush nests deep within the protected confines of vast hardwoods. Cowbirds, historically linked to the open fields, now parasitize this thrush's nests, depositing foreign eggs within its brood.

Like the hope and faith that seem to flow with the Wood Thrush's melody, the future might still hold promise for this often-glorified songbird. As pioneer farms are slowly abandoned and we learn to value the sanctity of a bird song, the wild spirit of the Wood Thrush offers up an optimistic note.

Similar Species: Veery (p. 99), Hermit Thrush and Swainson's Thrush all lack the bold black chest spots and reddish head.

Quick I.D.: smaller than a robin; sexes similar; plump; large, black spots on white breast; reddish-brown head; brown rump and tail; white eye ring.
Size: 7¹/₂–8¹/₂ in.

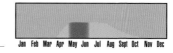

Jan Feb Mar Apr May Jun Jul Aug Sept Oct Nov Dec

American Robin
Turdus migratorius

If not for its abundance, the American Robin's voice and plumage would inspire pause and praise from casual onlookers. However, acclimatization has dealt the robin an unfair hand, and it is generally not fully appreciated for the pleasures it offers the eyes and ears of Chicago-area residents.

Nevertheless, the American Robin's close relationship with urban areas has allowed many residents an insight into a bird's life. A robin dashing around a yard in search of worms or ripe berries is as familiar to many people as its early pre-dawn, three-part *cheerily-cheery up-cheerio* song. American Robins also make up part of the emotional landscape of communities as their cheery song, their spotted young and occasionally even their deaths are experiences shared by their human neighbors.

American Robins are year-round residents in Chicago, but the bird dashing on your lawn in June might not be the same bird that shivers in February. Unnoticed by most residents, the neighborhood robins take seasonal shifts; new birds arrive from the north just when some summer residents depart for southern climes in fall.

Similar Species: Immature robins can be confused with other thrushes, but robins always have at least a hint of red in the breast.

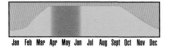

Quick I.D.: smaller than a jay; dark head, back and tail; yellow bill; striped throat; white under-tail coverts. *Male:* brick red breast; darker hood. *Female:* slightly more orange breast; lighter hood. **Size:** 9–11 in.

Warbling Vireo
Vireo gilvus

The Warbling Vireo can be quite common during the summer months, but you still need to make a prolonged search before spotting this bird. Lacking any splashy field marks, the Warbling Vireo is exceedingly difficult to spot unless it moves. Searching the treetops for this inconspicuous bird may be a 'pain in the neck,' but the satisfaction in visually confirming its identity can be rewarding.

The velvety voice of the Warbling Vireo contrasts sharply with its dull, nondescript plumage. The often-repeated *I love you, I love you, I love you Ma'am* song delights the listening forest with its oscillating quality. The phrases finish on an upbeat, as if the bird is asking a question of the wilds.

Similar Species: Red-eyed Vireo (p. 103) has a black-and-white eyebrow and a gray cap.

breeding

Quick I.D.: smaller than a sparrow; sexes similar; indistinct white eyebrow; no wing bars; olive-gray upperparts; greenish flanks; light underparts; gray crown.
Size: 4¹/₂–5¹/₂ in.

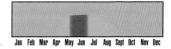

Jan Feb Mar Apr May Jun Jul Aug Sept Oct Nov Dec

Red-eyed Vireo
Vireo olivaceus

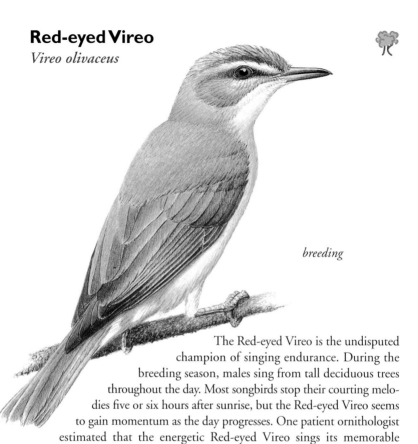

breeding

The Red-eyed Vireo is the undisputed champion of singing endurance. During the breeding season, males sing from tall deciduous trees throughout the day. Most songbirds stop their courting melodies five or six hours after sunrise, but the Red-eyed Vireo seems to gain momentum as the day progresses. One patient ornithologist estimated that the energetic Red-eyed Vireo sings its memorable phrase—*look up, way up, tree top, see me, here-I-am*—10,000 to 20,000 times a day.

Visual identification of the Red-eyed Vireo is much harder, because its olive-brown color conceals it well among the foliage of deciduous trees. Although this vireo does indeed have red eyes, this feature can only be seen through powerful binoculars in excellent light conditions.

Similar Species: Warbling Vireo (p. 102) is larger and lacks the black-and-white eyebrow.

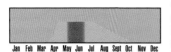

Jan Feb Mar Apr May Jun Jul Aug Sept Oct Nov Dec

Quick I.D.: sparrow-sized; sexes similar; gray crown bordered by black; white eyebrow; green back; white underparts; red eyes.
Size: 6 in.

Blue-winged Warbler
Vermivora pinus

There is nothing sinister to the thin, slick black eye line of this dainty little warbler; rather, its head gear adds an unusual high-tech style to this summer resident. This golden-bodied songbird has a song that is equally distinctive—its buzzy bellow ascends and then abruptly descends, like an inhaled-exhaled *bee-buzz*. These qualities can be experienced in May and June, during short walks around Ryerson Conservation Area, Cuba Marsh and Swallow Cliffs woods.

Blue-winged Warblers have also gained fame for their habit of breeding with other species. One of the few common examples of hybrids occur when this warbler interbreeds with the Golden-winged Warbler, producing the 'Brewster's Warbler.' This hybrid is found rarely in the Chicago area, and it occurs in far lesser numbers than its Blue-winged forebear.

Similar Species: Yellow Warbler (p. 106) lacks the black eye line and blue-gray wings. Golden-winged Warbler has a dark throat and white underparts. 'Brewster's Warbler' lacks the blue-gray wings and doesn't have as pure yellow underparts.

Quick I.D.: smaller than a sparrow; yellow body; black mask; blue-gray wings and tail; two merged white wing bars; dark legs. *Male:* brighter yellow on crown and nape. *Female:* yellow-green on head and nape; duller overall.
Size: 4–4¹/₂ in.

Jan Feb Mar Apr May Jun Jul Aug Sept Oct Nov Dec

Nashville Warbler
Vermivora ruficapilla

This common warbler has an identity crisis, not so much a result of its unassuming attire but because of its misleading name. If this small bird's name must reflect a place name, then the natural choice should be the 'Midwest Warbler.' A large part of this species's American breeding range is just to the north of us in Wisconsin, so its present name simply does not describe a location where it can be commonly found. The name seemed appropriate to Alexander Wilson when he collected the first specimen in Tennessee, but that bird was only passing through.

Such a misnomer is not an isolated incident, and many other warblers in Illinois bear the names given to them during migration. The Cape May (named for a site in New Jersey), Tennessee, Palm and Magnolia warblers are all northern-nesting species, but they bear names that do not reflect their breeding habits.

Nashville Warblers can be easily found fairly low in the flowering 'crabs' and hawthorns in our city parks and forest preserves.

Similar Species: Common Yellowthroat (p. 114) has a black mask. Connecticut Warbler is larger.

Quick I.D.: smaller than a sparrow; sexes similar; yellow underparts, from chin through undertail coverts; white vent; pale gray head and face; dark olive back; white eye ring.
Size: 5 in.

Jan Feb Mar Apr May Jun Jul Aug Sept Oct Nov Dec

VIREOS & WARBLERS 105

Yellow Warbler
Dendroica petechia

The Yellow Warbler is common in shrublands and in groves of alder, willow and cottonwood. As a consequence of its abundance, it is usually the first warbler birdwatchers identify in their lives, and every year thereafter. From mid-May through August, this brilliantly colored warbler is easily found in appropriate habitat throughout our area.

During our winters, Yellow Warblers migrate to the tropics, spending September to April in Mexico and South America. Following the first warm days of spring, the first of the Yellow Warblers return. Their distinctive courtship song—*sweet-sweet-sweet I'm so-so sweet*—is easily recognized in early May despite its eight-month absence. In true warbler fashion, the summertime activities of the Yellow Warbler are energetic and inquisitive, flitting from branch to branch in search of juicy caterpillars, aphids and beetles.

Similar Species: Wilson's Warbler has a small, black cap.

Quick I.D.: smaller than a sparrow; yellow overall; darker back, wings and tail; dark eyes and bill. *Male:* fine red streaking on breast. *Female:* no red streaking.
Size: 4–5 in.

Jan Feb Mar Apr May Jun Jul Aug Sept Oct Nov Dec

Chestnut-sided Warbler
Dendroica pensylvanica

breeding

Dropping down to human eye-level, the curious Chestnut-sided Warbler invites all into young deciduous stands with a hearty *so pleased pleased pleased to meet-cha* greeting. This woodland migrant appears genuinely hospitable, and in its flitty behavior it often passes within one branch of onlookers. Its distinctive chestnut-and-white belly accentuates the male warbler's timeless style for springtime fashion.

Chestnut-sided Warblers can be among the most common warblers in Chicago but only for a few weeks in spring and fall. Young, re-growing forests were far less common before colonization than they are today. Because of this change, it is now possible to see more Chestnut-sided Warblers in a single day during migration than some of the great pioneering naturalists saw in their entire lives.

Similar Species: Bay-breasted Warbler lacks the yellow crown and the white cheek and throat. Cape May Warbler lacks the white underparts.

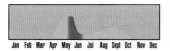

Jan Feb Mar Apr May Jun Jul Aug Sept Oct Nov Dec

Quick I.D.: smaller than a sparrow. *Breeding male:* white underparts; chestnut flanks; yellow crown; white cheek; light yellow wing bars; black and green–streaked back. *Breeding female:* less brilliant markings and colors.
Size: 5 in.

Yellow-rumped Warbler
Dendroica coronata

breeding

This spirited songbird is as common as it is delightful. Its contrasting colors, curiosity and tinkling trill are enthusiastically admired by even the most jaded birdwatcher. Yellow-rumped Warblers are the only year-round warbler in the Chicago area, with a few hardy individuals remaining to feed on poison ivy, juniper and hawthorn berries. However, it is not during the coldest months that Yellow-rumps are most noticeable; rather it is during late April and early May, when trees along the lakefront and forest preserves with water courses come alive with these colorful birds.

Most experienced birdwatchers continue to call these birds 'Myrtle Warblers.' Until fairly recently, our white-throated form was considered distinct from the western, yellow-throated form, the 'Audubon's Warbler.' This, however, has changed, resulting in the combined name of the Yellow-rumped Warbler.

Similar Species: Magnolia Warbler has yellow underparts and white patches in the tail.

Quick I.D.: smaller than a sparrow; blue-black back, tail and wings; yellow rump, crown and shoulder patches; white throat; faint white wing bars; dark chest band; white belly; dark cheek. *Male:* bright colors. *Female:* less intense colors.
Size: 5–6 in.

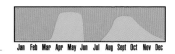

Jan Feb Mar Apr May Jun Jul Aug Sept Oct Nov Dec

Palm Warbler

Dendroica palmarum

For a few days each spring, large numbers of Palm Warblers pass through our area on route to their northern breeding grounds. Palm Warblers are lively transients; they can generally be found low in shrubs or hopping along trails and forest clearings gleaning for grasshoppers, beetles, moths and flies as comfortably as any sparrow. Their foraging behavior is surprisingly unique among the wood warblers, which as a group generally go about their foraging in trees and shrubs.

The Palm Warbler's yellow underparts gleam surprisingly in sunlight, while the dull red cap strikes a dark contrast. This warbler's most distinctive trait is perhaps its incessant habit of wagging its tail, regardless of whether it is perched or hopping along on the ground. Perhaps it should have been named for this wagging feature, because it is rarely seen among palms, even on its tropical wintering grounds.

Similar Species: Yellow-rumped Warbler (p. 108) has a yellow rump, darker upperparts and white wing bars. Chipping Sparrow (p. 123) has a stouter body, unstreaked underparts and no yellow in the plumage.

breeding

Jan Feb Mar Apr May Jun Jul Aug Sept Oct Nov Dec

Quick I.D.: sparrow-sized; sexes similar; chestnut cap; yellow throat and undertail coverts; streaked brown breast and belly; whitish-yellow eyebrow; olive-brown upperparts.
Size: 5¹/₂ in.

Black-and-white Warbler
Mniotilta varia

In general appearance, the Black-and-white Warbler seems quite normal, but its foraging behavior lies in sharp contrast to most of its warbler kin. Rather than dancing quickly between twig perches like most warblers, Black-and-white Warblers have a foraging strategy similar to an entirely unrelated group of birds—the nuthatches. As if possessed by nuthatch envy, Black-and-white Warblers hop gingerly up and down tree trunks in search of insect eggs, larval insects, beetles, spiders and other invertebrates.

Unfortunately, forest fragmentation and development in the Chicago area have forced breeding birds elsewhere. They do occur regularly throughout our area in migration, appearing in backyards and forest preserves and in Lincoln Park during their prolonged spring and fall passages. A novice birdwatcher can easily identify this two-toned and oddly behaved warbler. A keen ear also helps: the gentle oscillating song—like a wheel in need of greasing—is easily identified and remembered.

Similar Species: Blackpoll Warbler has orange legs and a solid black cap.

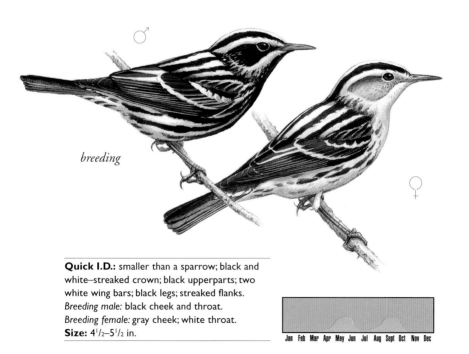

breeding

Quick I.D.: smaller than a sparrow; black and white–streaked crown; black upperparts; two white wing bars; black legs; streaked flanks.
Breeding male: black cheek and throat.
Breeding female: gray cheek; white throat.
Size: 4$\frac{1}{2}$–5$\frac{1}{2}$ in.

Jan Feb Mar Apr May Jun Jul Aug Sept Oct Nov Dec

American Redstart
Setophaga ruticilla

Like an over-energized wind-up toy, the American Redstart flits from branch to branch in a dizzying pursuit of prey. Never for a moment will a redstart pause; even while it's perched, its orange-splashed tail waves gently behind. This erratic and amusing behavior is easily observed in the bird's summering ground as well as its Central American wintering habitat, where it is affectionately known as *candelita* (the little candle). With constantly quivering wings, tail and shoulders, the redstart's patches are sparks of life in any dark forest.

Although American Redstarts breed sparingly in the Chicago area, their songs are so wonderfully various that even after a spring season is spent listening to them, their songs can still be confusing. While walking in any forest area in May, and in Ryerson Conservation Area, Swallow Cliff woods and Chain O'Lakes State Park in summer, you can discover the bird's energy and enthusiasm.

Similar Species: Red-winged Blackbird (p. 132) is much larger and has no red on its chest or tail.

Jan Feb Mar Apr May Jun Jul Aug Sept Oct Nov Dec

Quick I.D.: smaller than a sparrow. *Male:* black overall, with fiery orange patches in wings, tail and side of breast; white belly. *Female:* olive-brown back; light underparts; peach-yellow patches in wings and tail and on shoulders. **Size:** 5 in.

Ovenbird
Seiurus aurocapillus

The Ovenbird—or at least its song *teacher teacher Teacher TEACHER*—is a trademark of this bird's breeding habitat. Its loud and distinctive song announces its presence in deciduous woods, and its noisy habit of walking through the undergrowth nearly reveals its precise location. Despite having a good indication of the Ovenbird's location, this songbird's cryptic plumage and its stubborn refusal to become airborne frustrate many birders intent on a quick peek. Rarely will Ovenbirds expose themselves to the open forest; they seem most comfortable in the tangle of shrubs, stumps and dead leaves.

The sharp, loud call of the Ovenbird rises from the dense layer of shrubs and plants and is one of the most distinctive voices of Chicago-area forests. Unfortunately, our disappearing forests have also taken a toll on this special bird, because it continually yields forest patches in the face of development.

Similar Species: Wood Thrush (p. 100) is much larger and lacks the streaked russet-orange crown. Northern Waterthrush (p. 113) lacks the russet-orange crown stripe and has a light eyebrow.

Quick I.D.: sparrow-sized; sexes similar; heavily streaked breast; olive-brown back; russet-orange crown stripe bordered by black; pinkish legs.
Size: 6 in.

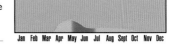

Jan Feb Mar Apr May Jun Jul Aug Sept Oct Nov Dec

Northern Waterthrush
Seiurus noveboracensis

The Northern Waterthrush is not much of a visual bird but rather a testament song of wet woods. Northern Waterthrushes are well recognized and admired through song—a loud staccato *chew chew chew chew where-where-where-where-where*—the quality of which seems perfectly suited to their inhospitable haunts. It, perhaps better than any other bird of the Chicago area, raises the need for aspiring bird lovers to learn the calls and songs of these creatures.

A first glimpse of this unusual warbler in its wet woodland haunts reminds birdwatchers of a Spotted Sandpiper. The teetering body and heavily spotted Northern Waterthrush bobbing around a puddle can be accidentally mistaken for these quite different birds. The Northern Waterthrush is a rather common migrant along the shorelines of Lake Michigan and along rivers in forest preserves, where these birds are often encountered in May and September.

Similar Species: Ovenbird (p. 112) lacks the eyebrow and has an eye ring. Louisiana Waterthrush has a whiter eyebrow extending to the nape and an unstreaked throat.

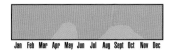

Jan Feb Mar Apr May Jun Jul Aug Sept Oct Nov Dec

Quick I.D.: sparrow-sized; sexes similar; solid brown upperparts; light, heavily streaked, yellowish underparts; yellowish eyebrow; dark eye line; streaked cheek; light-colored legs.
Size: 5¹/₂–6 in.

Common Yellowthroat
Geothlypis trichas

With so much diversity in North America's wood warbler clan, it is no surprise that one species has forsaken forests in favor of cattail marshes. The male Common Yellowthroat is easily identified by his black mask or by his oscillating *witchety-witchety-witchety* song. In our area, this energetic warbler reaches its highest abundance along wetland brambles and cattails, but it can be seen and heard along the vegetation bordering many freshwater marshes.

Female yellowthroats are rarely seen because they keep to their nests, deep within the thick vegetation surrounding marshes. The Common Yellowthroat's nests are often parasitized by Brown-headed Cowbirds. Should the nest avoid these common nest parasites, three to five young hatch after only about 12 days of incubation. These young continue their rapid development, soon leaving the nest and allowing the parents to repeat the process once again.

Similar Species: Male is distinct. Female Nashville Warbler (p. 105) has dark brown legs and an eye ring.

Quick I.D.: smaller than a sparrow; pinkish legs; yellow throat and underparts; olive upperparts.
Male: black mask; white border on forehead.
Female: no mask.
Size: 4¹/₂–5¹/₂ in.

Jan Feb Mar Apr May Jun Jul Aug Sept Oct Nov Dec

Scarlet Tanager
Piranga olivacea

breeding

♂

The tropical appearance of the Scarlet Tanager's plumage reinforces the link between the forests of South America and eastern North America. A winter resident of the tropics and a breeder in Chicago's mixed-woods, this tanager is vulnerable to deforestation at both extremes of its range.

Scarlet Tanagers can be difficult to see despite their tropical wardrobe, because they tend to sing their throaty, robin-like warble—*hurry-worry-lurry-scurry*—from high up in deciduous forest canopies. Because its song has the same quality as a robin's song, the tanager is frequently disregarded as a common woodland voice. Novice birdwatchers should listen for its hiccup-like *chick-burr* call as it cascades to the forest floor.

The Scarlet Tanager is one of Chicago's most breathtaking birds, and every brief encounter is sure to make you wish that the meeting might have lasted just a little longer.

Similar Species: Northern Cardinal (p. 139), Baltimore Oriole (p. 136) and Orchard Oriole lack the combination of an all-red body and black wings.

Jan Feb Mar Apr May Jun Jul Aug Sept Oct Nov Dec

Quick I.D.: smaller than a robin.
Male: unmistakable, magnificent scarlet body with contrasting black wings and tail; changes in fall to look like female. *Female:* olive-yellow overall; pale brownish flight feathers.
Size: 6¹/₂–7¹/₂ in.

Horned Lark
Eremophila alpestris

Horned Larks are probably most frequently encountered rising up in front of vehicles speeding along country roads. They cut off to the side an instant before a fatal collision, briefly showing off their distinct black outer tail feathers. Horned Larks resort to these near misses because their first instinct when threatened is to outrun their pursuer. Cars can easily overtake these swift runners, however, so these birds take to the air when their first attempt to flee fails.

Late winter is the best time of year to observe these open-country specialists as they congregate in huge flocks on outlying farmland, eating waste grain. Most of these birds are destined to migrate north when the first hints of warmth loosens winter's chilly grip. However, this migration does not mean that our area is free of these birds through summer, because many nest in our open fields and pastures. They are among the earliest of our courting birds, singing their songs and diving dare-devilishly before the snow has all retreated.

Similar Species: Sparrows lack the black facial and throat markings.

Quick I.D.: larger than a sparrow; brown plumage; black bib, mask and 'tiara'; light underparts; white outer edges on black tail feathers; faint yellow throat. *Female:* duller overall; less prominent horns.
Size: 7–8 in.

Jan Feb Mar Apr May Jun Jul Aug Sept Oct Nov Dec

European Starling
Sturnus vulgaris

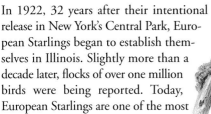

breeding

In 1922, 32 years after their intentional release in New York's Central Park, European Starlings began to establish themselves in Illinois. Slightly more than a decade later, flocks of over one million birds were being reported. Today, European Starlings are one of the most common birds in Chicago. Their presence is highlighted by astonishing numbers roosting communally during the winter months.

Unfortunately, the expansion of starlings has come at the expense of many of our native birds, including the Purple Martin and the Eastern Bluebird, which are unable to defend nest cavities against the aggressive starlings. While not all birdwatchers are pleased with the presence of this foreigner to our area, starlings have become a permanent fixture in the bird community. If residents are unable to find joy in this bird's mimicry and flocking, they can take some comfort in knowing that starlings now provide a reliable and stable food source for woodland hawks and the Peregrine Falcon.

Similar Species: All blackbirds have long tails and black bills. Purple Martin (p. 85) has a short bill.

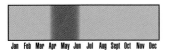

Jan Feb Mar Apr May Jun Jul Aug Sept Oct Nov Dec

Quick I.D.: smaller than a robin; sexes similar; short tail. *Breeding:* dark, glossy plumage; long, yellow bill. *Non-breeding:* dark bill; spotty plumage. *Juvenile:* brown upperparts; gray-brown underparts; brown bill.
Size: 8–9 in.

MID-SIZED SONGBIRDS 117

Gray Catbird
Dumetella carolinensis

The Gray Catbird is a sleek bird that commonly displays an unusual 'mooning' behavior: it raises its long, slender tail to show its chestnut undertail coverts. This behavior is one of the elements of courtship, and the coverts might help female catbirds to choose the best mates.

The Gray Catbird is a bird of dense shrubs and thickets, and although it's relatively common in appropriate habitats, its distinctive call, rather than the bird itself, is what is most commonly encountered. The Gray Catbird's unmistakable cat-like 'meowing,' for which it's named, can be heard rising from shrubs in forest preserves and shrubby thickets anywhere in our area during May and June.

Similar Species: None.

Quick I.D.: smaller than a robin; sexes similar; slate gray; black cap; chestnut undertail coverts; long, dark tail.
Size: 9 in.

Jan Feb Mar Apr May Jun Jul Aug Sept Oct Nov Dec

Brown Thrasher

Toxostoma rufum

Male Brown Thrashers have the largest vocal repertoire of any Chicago-area bird—more than 3000 song types. Although thrashers don't have the sweetest voice in Chicago, their loud, continually varying songs are worth listening to. Thrashers will repeat phrases twice, often combining them into complex choruses, such as *dig-it dig-it, hoe-it hoe-it, pull-it-up pull-it-up.*

Brown Thrashers have a reddish-brown back and tail and a heavily streaked breast. They're common in thickets and shrubs, often in close proximity to humans. They're shy birds, however, and they need a lot of coaxing with squeaks and pishes before they pop out into the open. Illinois Beach State Park, during summer, offers ample opportunity to meet this dynamic songster.

Similar Species: Wood Thrush (p. 100) and Veery (p. 99) have shorter tails and straight bills.

Jan Feb Mar Apr May Jun Jul Aug Sept Oct Nov Dec

Quick I.D.: jay-sized; sexes similar; reddish-brown head, back and tail; heavy chest streaking; long, downcurved bill; white wing bars; long tail; no eye ring; yellow eyes.
Size: 11–12 in.

Cedar Waxwing
Bombycilla cedrorum

A faint, high-pitched trill is often your first clue that waxwings are around. Search the treetops to see these cinnamon-crested birds as they dart out in quick bursts, snacking on flying insects. Cedar Waxwings are found in many habitats throughout Chicago, wherever ripe berries provide abundant food supplies.

Cedar Waxwings are most often seen in large flocks in late spring and fall, when they congregate on fruit trees and quickly eat all the berries. Some people remember these visits not only for the birds' beauty, but because fermentation of the fruit occasionally renders the flock flightless from intoxication.

Similar Species: Tufted Titmouse has no yellow on its belly or tail.

Quick I.D.: smaller than a robin; sexes similar; fine, pale brown plumage; small crest; black mask; yellow belly wash; yellow-tipped tail; light under-tail coverts; shiny red (waxy-looking) droplets on wing tips. *Juvenile:* streaky underparts.
Size: 7–8 in.

Jan Feb Mar Apr May Jun Jul Aug Sept Oct Nov Dec

Eastern Towhee
Pipilo erythrophthalmus

This large, cocky sparrow is most often heard before it is seen, scratching away leaves and debris in the dense understory. These are noisy foragers, because Eastern Towhees tend to make the most out of leaf litter scattered beneath second-growth deciduous areas. Deep in the shadows of shrubs, the Eastern Towhee's sharp, *Drink your Teeea* identifies this secretive sparrow.

To best observe this bird, which was formerly grouped with the West's Spotted Towhee (together they were known as the Rufous-sided Towhee), learn a few birding tricks. Squeaking and pishing are irresistible for towhees, which will quickly pop out from the cover to investigate the curious noise.

Similar Species: American Robin (p. 101) is larger and has no white on its chest. Dark-eyed Junco (p. 130) is smaller and has white outer tail feathers.

Jan Feb Mar Apr May Jun Jul Aug Sept Oct Nov Dec

Quick I.D.: smaller than a robin; black head; rufous-colored flanks; black back; white outer tail feathers; white underparts; red eyes.
Male: black head, breast and upperparts.
Female: reddish-brown head, breast and upperparts.
Size: 8–9 in.

American Tree Sparrow
Spizella arborea

The American Tree Sparrow's annual migration into Illinois during late fall is a sign of the changing seasons. For the entire winter, these Arctic nesters decorate the leafless rural shrublands like ornaments on a Christmas tree. As one of the first songbirds to disappear in April and a regular arrival in late October, American Tree Sparrow activities quietly announce the closing of autumn and the opening of spring.

These humble, quiet sparrows often go unnoticed despite their large numbers. American Tree Sparrows occasionally visit city feeders during their migrations and while wintering in the Chicago area, but they never attempt to usurp the surly resident flocks of House Sparrows and House Finches, because these sparrows prefer outlying weedy and fallow fields.

Similar Species: Chipping (p. 123), Field (p. 124) and Swamp (p. 128) sparrows all lack a faint breast spot.

Quick I.D.: large sparrow; sexes similar; red crown; no eyebrow; small, central chest spot, breast otherwise unstreaked; mottled back; grayish bill with yellow lower mandible; white wing bars.
Size: 6 in.

Jan Feb Mar Apr May Jun Jul Aug Sept Oct Nov Dec

Chipping Sparrow

Spizella passerina

Hopping around freshly mowed lawns, the cheery Chipping Sparrow goes about its business unconcerned by the busy world of suburban Chicago. One of the most widespread species in Illinois, the Chipping Sparrow brings birdwatching to those who rarely venture from their homes.

These sparrows nest frequently in our backyards, building their small nest cups with dried vegetation and lining them with animal hair. Chipping Sparrows usually attempt to bring off two broods of young every year in Chicago. Three or four small, greenish-blue eggs are laid in mid-May, and again later near the beginning of July, should conditions prove favorable. These passive birds are delightful neighbors in our backyards, and they demand nothing more than a little privacy around the rose bush, vine tangle or small tree where they have chosen to nest.

Similar Species: American Tree Sparrow (p. 122) is only a winter resident and has a black central chest spot. Swamp Sparrow (p. 128) lacks the clean white, black-lined eyebrow. Field Sparrow (p. 124) has a pink bill and lacks the white eyebrow.

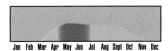

Jan Feb Mar Apr May Jun Jul Aug Sept Oct Nov Dec

Quick I.D.: small sparrow; sexes similar; red crown; white eyebrow; black eye line; clear grayish breast; streaked back.
Size: 5 1/2 in.

Field Sparrow
Spizella pusilla

The innocent, unmarked face of the Field Sparrow gives this common bird a perpetual look of adolescence. Like a teenager prior to his first shave, the Field Sparrow has a soft, wholesome look, highlighted by its pink bill and untainted eyes.

Many sparrows have very descriptive and accurate names, but the Field Sparrow's name is somewhat misleading. An inhabitant of overgrown meadows and bushy areas, Field Sparrows tend to avoid expansive, grassy fields. Their nesting sites are often found away from developments, but not far enough from Brown-headed Cowbirds. These nest parasites can occupy over one-quarter of the nests in our area, affecting the Field Sparrow's reproductive rate. Fortunately, cowbirds have not significantly decreased the population of these tireless singers, who offer their 'ping pong ball' song on hot summer days when most other singers are silenced.

Similar Species: Chipping Sparrow (p. 123) has a white eyebrow and a black eye line. American Tree Sparrow (p. 122) has a dark chest spot and a dark bill.

Quick I.D.: mid-sized sparrow; sexes similar; reddish crown; plain gray underparts; pink bill; light gray eyebrow; rusty brown back; prominent white eye ring.
Size: 5–6 in.

Jan Feb Mar Apr May Jun Jul Aug Sept Oct Nov Dec

Savannah Sparrow
Passerculus sandwichensis

The Savannah Sparrow is a common bird of the open country. Its dull brown plumage and streaked breast conceal it perfectly in the long grasses of native prairie, farms and roadsides. It breeds in fields of weedy annuals and grass along Vollmer Road and in grassy rural areas.

The Savannah Sparrow resorts to flight only as a last alternative: it prefers to run swiftly and inconspicuously through long grass, and it is most often seen darting across roads and open fields. The Savannah Sparrow's distinctive buzzy trill—*tea-tea-tea-teeea today*—and the usual yellow eyebrow and patch in front of each eye are the best ways to distinguish it from the many other grassland sparrows.

Similar Species: Song Sparrow (p. 127) has a breast spot. Vesper Sparrow lacks the yellow lore, has white outer tail feathers and a chestnut shoulder patch, and its song is a buzzy *Here here, there there, Everybody down the hill.*

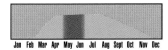

Jan Feb Mar Apr May Jun Jul Aug Sept Oct Nov Dec

Quick I.D.: small sparrow; sexes similar; streaked underparts and upperparts; mottled brown above; dark cheek; no white outer tail feathers; usually has yellow lores.
Size: 5–6 in.

Fox Sparrow
Passerella iliaca

The Fox Sparrow is a noisy migrant in Chicago's thickets and brambles. Like many other sparrows that spend time in this habitat, the Fox Sparrow is appreciated for its voice more than for its subtle, beautiful plumage. During spring, sit and wait near tangles and brush piles in Chicago's parks, and listen as the Fox Sparrow repeatedly belts out its distinctive musical question: *All I have is what's here dear, will-you-will-you take-it?*

The Fox Sparrow hops under feeders and shrubs noisily scratching at leaf litter like a towhee. It finds these areas to its liking, and this bird is infrequently seen anywhere in our region farther than a quick getaway flight into bushes.

Similar Species: Song Sparrow (p. 127) has a different song and a much lighter color. Hermit Thrush has a slimmer bill and smaller breast spots and lacks the gray in the head.

Quick I.D.: large sparrow; sexes similar; heavy breast streaks; red-brown tail, wings and back; light gray-brown head and nape; very dark overall.
Size: 6¹/₂–7 in.

Jan Feb Mar Apr May Jun Jul Aug Sept Oct Nov Dec

Song Sparrow
Melospiza melodia

The Song Sparrow's drab, heavily streaked plumage doesn't prepare you for its symphonic song, which stands out among Chicago-area songsters in complexity and rhythm. This bird, Chicago's most common native sparrow, seems to sing *hip-hip-hip hooray boys, the spring is here again..*

This year-round resident is encountered in a wide variety of habitats. Song Sparrows are easily found in all seasons among marshes, thickets, brambles, weedy fields and woodland edges. Although these birds are most easily identified by their grayish facial streaks while perched, flying birds will characteristically pump their tails.

Similar Species: Fox Sparrow (p. 126) is very heavily streaked and has a different song. Savannah Sparrow (p. 125) and Lincoln's Sparrow have weaker breast streaks.

Jan Feb Mar Apr May Jun Jul Aug Sept Oct Nov Dec

Quick I.D.: mid-sized sparrow; sexes similar; heavy breast streaks form central spot; brown-red plumage; striped head.
Size: 6–7 in.

Swamp Sparrow
Melospiza georgiana

breeding

Although Swamp Sparrows are fairly common in wetlands in the Chicago area, they are far less visible than their neighboring blackbirds and yellowthroats. Except when the male pounces atop a bulrush or willow branch to sing his sweet, loose trill, the Swamp Sparrow seems perfectly content sealed deep within the world of cattail and grasses.

Swamp Sparrows are the most adaptive of the sparrows in our area to life around water. Like all other sparrows, they are unable to swim, but that is no deterrent to this rufous-crowned skulker. Swamp Sparrows glean much of their insectivorous diet directly from the surface of wetlands, and they construct their sideways nest just a foot above the water line. As if Swamp Sparrows become bored with their concealed lifestyle, they can be readily enticed to quickly pop up to a cattail head in response to a birder's urging squeaks.

Similar Species: Chipping Sparrow (p. 123) has a clean white eyebrow, a black eye line and uniform gray underparts. American Tree Sparrow (p. 122) has a central dark chest spot and a two-toned bill.

Quick I.D.: mid-sized sparrow; sexes similar; gray face; rufous upperparts and wings; streaked back. *Breeding:* red cap; white throat; light gray breast; reddish-brown underparts. *Non-breeding:* streaked, brown cap.
Size: 5¹/₂ in.

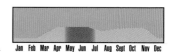

Jan Feb Mar Apr May Jun Jul Aug Sept Oct Nov Dec

White-throated Sparrow
Zonotrichia albicollis

The catchy song of the White-throated Sparrow is often on the lips of weekend cottagers returning from the north country. By whistling the distinctive *Oh sweet Canada Canada Canada* to themselves, people bring some of the atmosphere of the northern woods to their Chicago-area homes.

In winter, a few White-throated Sparrows linger in the city, where birdfeeders provide them with a steady supply of seed without much physical exertion. This bird's striped head and white throat, as well as its wild song ringing in the steep-walled skyscraper canyons during our winter, allow this forest breeder to stand out.

Similar Species: White-crowned Sparrow lacks the white throat and has a pink bill.

Quick I.D.: large sparrow; sexes similar; black and white–striped head; white throat; unstreaked, light gray breast; yellow lore; rusty-brown upperparts; tan phase has brownish, rather than white, streaks on head.
Size: 6¹/₂–7 in.

Jan Feb Mar Apr May Jun Jul Aug Sept Oct Nov Dec

Dark-eyed Junco
Junco hyemalis

Dark-eyed Juncos occur as abundant migrants and winter visitors throughout the Chicago area. The Dark-eyed Junco is a ground dweller, and it is frequently seen as it flushes from the undergrowth along wooded trails in Chicago's parks and under suburban shrubbery. The distinctive white outer tail feathers will flash in alarm as the bird flies down a narrow path before disappearing into a thicket.

In spring, Dark-eyed Juncos sing their descending trills, which are often easily mistaken with those of the Chipping Sparrow. The confusion can build, because both the junco and the sparrow occur in similar habitats, so a confirmation of identity usually requires a visual search. The junco's distinctive smacking call and its habit of double-scratching at forest litter also help identify it. Juncos are frequent guests at birdfeeders throughout Chicago, usually cleaning up the forgotten seed that has fallen to the ground.

Similar Species: Eastern Towhee (p. 121) is larger and has conspicuous rufous sides. Brown-headed Cowbird (p. 135) lacks the white outer tail feathers and white belly.

Quick I.D.: large sparrow; slate gray; light-colored bill; white outer tail feathers; white belly. *Female:* somewhat duller.
Size: 5–6¹/₂ in.

Jan Feb Mar Apr May Jun Jul Aug Sept Oct Nov Dec

Bobolink
Dolichonyx oryzivorus

During spring, small flocks of Bobolinks return to alfalfa and hayfields in our area. The males arrive a few days before the females and perform their bubbly, tinkly song *bob-o-link bob-o-link, spink, spank, spink,* assuring farmers and naturalists that spring is here to stay. Their vigilance is short-lived: their plumage and attitude soon fade when summer wanes and the fields turn gold.

At first glimpse, Bobolinks look every bit a sparrow, especially the drab females, which lack the male's style—he looks as though he's wearing a tuxedo backwards. But these are not sparrows at all; rather, they are blackbirds— evident by their polygynous breeding strategy. Males that acquire prime hayfields can mate with and defend several nesting females.

The fall migration of Bobolinks is one of the most spectacular and longest of all songbirds. Birds leaving Illinois flock with others farther south and soon number in the thousands. These flocks once descended on rice crops in the southeast states, where they were known as 'rice birds.' Bobolinks were so effectively controlled by rice farmers and the elimination of hayfields and prairie remnants that the populations that occur in the Chicago area continue to recover to this day.

Similar Species: Brown-headed Cowbird (p. 135) has a black back. Sparrows tend to lack the pointy tail feathers.

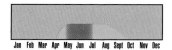

Jan Feb Mar Apr May Jun Jul Aug Sept Oct Nov Dec

Quick I.D.: larger than a sparrow; pointed tail feathers. *Breeding male:* black head and body; buffy nape; white rump. *Female* and *Non-breeding male:* buffy brown body; dark crown streaks; dark eye line.
Size: 6–8 in.

Red-winged Blackbird

Agelaius phoeniceus

From March through July, no marsh is free from the loud calls and bossy, aggressive nature of the Red-winged Blackbird. A springtime walk around any Chicago-area marshland will be accompanied by this bird's loud, raspy and persistent *konk-a-reee* or *eat my CHEEEzies* song. During fall migration, the shorelines of Lake Michigan can become congested with thousands of these birds as they flock their way southwards.

The male's bright red shoulders (or 'epaulets') are his most important tool in the strategic and intricate displays he uses to defend his territory from rivals and to attract a mate. In experiments, males whose red shoulders were painted black soon lost their territories to rivals they had previously defeated. The female's interest lies not in the individual combatants, but in nesting habitat, and a male that can successfully defend a large area of dense cattails will breed with many females. After the females have built their concealed nests and laid their eggs, the male continues his persistent vigil.

Similar Species: Brewer's Blackbird and Brown-headed Cowbird (p. 135) lack the red shoulder patches.

Quick I.D.: smaller than a robin. *Male:* all-black plumage; large, red patch bordered by creamy yellow on each shoulder. *Female:* brown overall; heavily streaked; hint of red on shoulder.
Size: 7¹/₂–9¹/₂ in.

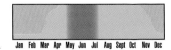

Jan Feb Mar Apr May Jun Jul Aug Sept Oct Nov Dec

Eastern Meadowlark
Sturnella magna

breeding

Eastern Meadowlarks are well adapted to the landscape of the fields and pastures where they spend their summers. In our area, the flute-like melody song—*This is the Year of the meadowlark*—is a signature of open-country farmlands, fallow fields and airports.

Eastern Meadowlarks are both showy and perfectly camouflaged. Their yellow sweater with the black V-neck and their white outer tail feathers serve to attract mates—and predators. Potential meadowlark mates face one another, raise their bills high and perform a grassland ballet. Oddly, the colorful breast and white tail feathers are also used to attract the attention of potential predators. Foxes, hawks or falcons focus on these bold features in pursuit, so their prey mysteriously disappears into the grass whenever the meadowlark chooses to turn its back or fold away its white tail flags.

Similar Species: Savannah Sparrow (p. 125) is much smaller and lacks the yellow chest and white outer tail feathers. Dickcissel (p. 142) is smaller and lacks the white outer tail feathers. Western Meadowlark lacks the dark reddish-brown upperparts.

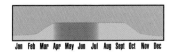

Jan Feb Mar Apr May Jun Jul Aug Sept Oct Nov Dec

Quick I.D.: robin-sized; sexes similar; mottled brown upperparts; black 'V' on chest; yellow throat and belly; white outer tail feathers; striped head.
Size: 8–10 in.

Common Grackle
Quiscalus quiscula

The Common Grackle is a noisy and cocky bird that prefers to feed on the ground in open areas. Birdfeeders in rural areas can attract large numbers of these blackish birds, whose cranky disposition drives away most other birds (even the quarrelsome Blue Jay and House Sparrow). The Common Grackle is easily identified by its long tail, large bill and dark plumage, which can shine with hues of green, purple and blue in bright light.

The Common Grackle is a poor but spirited singer. Usually while perched in a shrub, a male grackle will slowly take a deep breath that inflates his chest and causes his feathers to rise. Then he closes his eyes and gives out a loud, surprising *swaaaack*. Despite our perception of the Common Grackle's musical weakness, following his 'song' the male smugly and proudly poses with his bill held high, to display his dominance.

Similar Species: Brown-headed Cowbird (p. 135), American Crow (p. 90) and Rusty Blackbird have relatively shorter tails.

Quick I.D.: jay-sized; sexes similar; glossy black plumage with purple and brown iridescence; long, keeled tail; large bill.
Size: 11–13 in.

Brown-headed Cowbird

Molothrus ater

Brown-headed Cowbirds have been well established within the matrix of the region's bird life since they followed the historic wanderings of bison. This gregarious bird is very common in outlying agricultural areas, and it can be seen in large numbers during migration along Lake Michigan.

The Brown-headed Cowbird is infamous for being a nest parasite—female cowbirds do not incubate their own eggs, but instead lay them in the nests of many songbirds. Cowbird eggs have a short incubation period, and the cowbird chicks often hatch before the host songbird's own chicks. Many songbirds do not recognize that the fast-growing cowbird chick is not one of their own, and they will continue to feed it even after the cowbird chick has grown larger than the songbird. In its efforts to get as much food as possible, a cowbird chick might squeeze the host's own young out of the nest. The populations of many songbird species in Illinois have been devastated in part by the activities of the Brown-headed.

Similar Species: Common Grackle (p. 134) has a relatively longer tail. Rusty Blackbird has a slimmer body and yellow eyes.

Quick I.D.: smaller than a robin. *Male:* metallic-looking, glossy black plumage; soft brown head; dark eyes. *Female:* brownish gray overall; dark eyes; slight chest streaks.
Size: 6–8 in.

Baltimore Oriole
Icterus galbula

Although it is a common summer resident of city parks and cottonwood and willow valleys, the Baltimore Oriole is seldom seen. Unlike the American Robin, which inhabits the human domain of shrubs and lawns, the Baltimore Oriole nests and feeds in the tallest deciduous trees available. The vacant nest, which is easily seen on bare trees in fall, is often the only indication that a pair of orioles summered in an area. This bird's hanging, six-inch-deep, pouch-like nest is deceptively strong.

The male Baltimore Oriole's striking, Halloween-like, black-and-orange plumage flashes like embers amidst the dense foliage of the treetops, while its slow purposeful *Peter Peter here here Peter Peter* song drips to the forest floor.

From mid-May to mid-July, mature deciduous forests or second-growth parkland throughout our area should produce at least one of these beautiful birds for oriole-starved Chicago-area birdwatchers.

Similar Species: Orchard Oriole is smaller and has chestnut rather than orange plumage.

Quick I.D.: smaller than a robin. *Male:* brilliant orange belly, flanks, outer tail feathers and rump; black hood, wings and tail. *Female:* yellow-green upperparts; yellow throat; faint hood.
Size: 7–8 in.

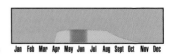

Jan Feb Mar Apr May Jun Jul Aug Sept Oct Nov Dec

House Finch
Carpodacus mexicanus

The House Finch is one of the earliest voices to announce the coming of spring. These common city and country birds sing their warbling melodies from backyards, parks and suburban TV antennas.

During the 1920s and 1930s, these birds, native to the American Southwest, were popular cage birds, and they were sold across the continent as 'Hollywood Finches.' Illegal releases of the caged birds and expansion from their historic range have resulted in two separate distributions in North America, which have recently converged. House Finches found in Illinois spread from the east and arrived in 1972. They are now well established here, nesting in house gutters and flower baskets.

Similar Species: Male Purple Finch is raspberry-colored and has unstreaked undertail coverts, and the female has a brown cheek contrasting with a white eyebrow and a mustache stripe.

Quick I.D.: sparrow-sized; squared tail. *Male:* deep red forehead, eyebrow and throat; buffy gray belly; brown cheek; streaked sides and undertail coverts. *Female:* brown overall; streaked underparts; no eyebrow.
Size: 5–6 in.

Jan Feb Mar Apr May Jun Jul Aug Sept Oct Nov Dec

American Goldfinch
Carduelis tristis

breeding

In spring, the American Goldfinch swings over fields in its distinctive, undulating flight, and it fills the air with its jubilant *po-ta-to chip* call. This bright, cheery songbird is commonly seen during summer in weedy fields, roadsides and backyards, where it feeds on thistle seeds. The American Goldfinch delays nesting until June or July to ensure a dependable source of insects, thistles and dandelion seeds to feed its young.

The American Goldfinch is a common backyard bird in parts of the Chicago area, and it can be attracted to feeding stations that offer a supply of niger seed. Goldfinches are easily bullied at feeders by larger sparrows and finches, but only goldfinches and Pine Siskins invert for food, so a special finch feeder with openings below the perches is ideal for ensuring a steady stream of what some people call 'wild canaries.'

Similar Species: Yellow Warbler (p. 106) does not have black on its forehead or wings. Evening Grosbeak is much larger and has broad white wing patches.

Quick I.D.: smaller than a sparrow. *Breeding male:* black forehead, wings and tail; canary yellow body; wings show white in flight. *Female and Non-breeding male:* no black on forehead; yellow-green overall; black wings and tail.
Size: 4¹/₂–5¹/₂ in.

Jan Feb Mar Apr May Jun Jul Aug Sept Oct Nov Dec

Northern Cardinal
Cardinalis cardinalis

The gallantry of the Northern Cardinal is not only found in its renowned attire—this species's pair bond is one of the most faithful of Chicago's resident birds. Never far from one another, male and female cardinals softly vocalize to one another not only through the breeding season, but year-round, as if sharing sweet nothings. The ritualized beak-to-beak feeding re-inforces the romantic appeal of these easily identifiable birds. Although the regal male does little more than warble to the female while she constructs the nest, his parental duties will soon keep him busy. After the eggs have hatched, the nestlings and the brooding female will remain in the nest while the male provides much of the food for the family.

The state bird of Illinois is common at backyard feeders. As if grateful to residents with backyard feeders, Northern Cardinals offer up their bubbly *What cheer! What cheer! Birdie-birdie-birdie What cheer!* and enliven neighborhoods.

Similar Species: Scarlet Tanager (p. 115) has black wings and tail.

Jan Feb Mar Apr May Jun Jul Aug Sept Oct Nov Dec

Quick I.D.: smaller than a robin. *Male:* unmistakable; red overall; black mask and throat; pointed crest; red, conical bill. *Female:* similar to male, except plumage quite a bit duller.
Size: 8–9 in.

Rose-breasted Grosbeak
Pheucticus ludovicianus

Male Rose-breasted Grosbeaks have a voice that matches their magnificent plumage. Showing not the least concern for would-be predators, male Rose-breasted Grosbeaks flaunt their song and plumage in treetop performances. This common songster's boldness does not go unnoticed by the appreciative birding community, which eagerly anticipates the male's annual spring concert. The male's outlandish plumage compensates for that of his unassuming mate, which lacks the formal dress but shares her partner's musical talents. Whether the nest is incubated by the male or female, the developing young are continually introduced into the world of song by the brooding parent.

This neotropical migrant nests in mature deciduous forest and second-growth shrubby areas, such as those found in parts of Ryerson Conservation Area or in less developed urban areas.

Similar Species: Male is distinctive. Female is similar to female Purple Finch and sparrows, but is generally larger.

Quick I.D.: smaller than a robin. *Male:* black hood; rose breast; black back and wings; white rump; white wing bars; light-colored, conical bill. *Female:* heavily streaked with brown; white eyebrow; pinkish or whitish, conical bill; light throat. **Size:** 7–8 in.

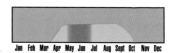

Jan Feb Mar Apr May Jun Jul Aug Sept Oct Nov Dec

Indigo Bunting
Passerina cyanea

Metallic-blue male Indigo Buntings are frequently encountered singing all day long along open areas of overgrown fields and forest edges. Perched atop a shrub or thicket, the males conduct elaborate tactical maneuvers with song. With rival males only a voice away, Indigo Buntings call continuously through the day to maintain superiority over their peers. Neighboring males copy and learn from one another, producing 'song territories.' Each male within a song territory has personal variation to *fire-fire, where-where, here-here, see-it see-it*, producing his own acoustic fingerprint.

Indigo Buntings are widespread throughout our area during summer, popping out of dense bushes anywhere along roadsides and park edges. They build a small nest cup low to the ground, in an upright crotch amid a shrubby tangle. Once nesting duties are complete, these buntings are commonly seen along railroad tracks, beginning their exodus in August, following a partial molt.

Similar Species: Eastern Bluebird (p. 98) is larger, has a red breast and slimmer body, and lacks the wing bars. Female is similar to many female sparrows, but lacks the streaking.

Quick I.D.: sparrow-sized; conical bill.
Male: turquoise blue plumage; darker wings and tail. *Female:* soft brown overall; hints of blue on rump.
Size: 5¹/₂ in.

Jan Feb Mar Apr May Jun Jul Aug Sept Oct Nov Dec

Dickcissel

Spiza americana

♂

breeding

♀

In an affectionate comparison of habitat, dress and behavior, the bright Dickcissel is often referred to as a mini-meadowlark. Like its much larger prairie ally, the Dickcissel can be seen singing atop posts and perches along the open country of Vollmer Road. Turning your ear in spring to the surrounding fields, you will be treated to the tell-tale song of the bird, an onomatopoeic *dick dick ciss, ciss ciss ...*

This distinctive song is easily heard throughout late spring, because this grassland-lover sings into the heat of the day, long after its chorus mates have been silenced. When Dickcissels' intentions veer away from reproduction and their singing stops, the fields once dominated by these large sparrows seem perfectly empty. At this time of year it is only when Dickcissels pass overhead that they are easily noticed, because they continually produce an electric buzzer–like *bzrrrt!*

Similar Species: Eastern Meadowlark (p. 133) is larger overall and has white outer tail feathers.

Quick I.D.: large sparrow; yellow eyebrow and breast; gray cheek; heavy bill; mottled brown back; chestnut shoulder; dark legs. *Male:* black bib. *Female:* duller overall; no black bib.
Size: 6–7 in.

Jan Feb Mar Apr May Jun Jul Aug Sept Oct Nov Dec

House Sparrow
Passer domesticus

This common backyard bird often confuses novice birdwatchers because females and immatures can be very nondescript. The male is relatively conspicuous—he has a black bib, a gray cap and white lines trailing down from his mouth (as though he has spilled milk on himself)—and he sings a continuous series of *cheep-cheep-cheeps*. The best field mark for the female, apart from her pale eyebrows, is that there are no distinctive field marks.

The House Sparrow was introduced to North America in the 1850s to control insects. Although this familiar bird can consume great quantities of insects, the majority of its diet is seeds, and it has become somewhat of a pest. The House Sparrow's aggressive nature usurps several native songbird species from nesting cavities, and its boldness often drives other birds away from backyard feeders. The House Sparrow and the European Starling are now two of the most common birds in cities and on farms, and they are a constant reminder of the negative impact of human introductions on natural systems.

Similar Species: Male is distinctive. Female is similar to female sparrows and finches, but tends to lack any distinctive markings.

Quick I.D.: mid-sized sparrow; brownish-gray belly. *Male:* black throat; gray forehead; white jowl; chestnut nape. *Female:* plain; pale eyebrow; mottled wings.
Size: 5¹/₂–6¹/₂ in.

Jan Feb Mar Apr May Jun Jul Aug Sept Oct Nov Dec

Watching Birds

Identifying your first new bird can be so satisfying that you just might become addicted to birdwatching. Luckily, birdwatching does not have to be expensive; it all hinges on how involved in this hobby you want to get. Setting up a simple backyard feeder is an easy way to get to know the birds sharing your neighborhood, and some people simply find birdwatching a pleasant way to complement a nightly walk with the dog or a morning commute into work.

Many people enjoy going to urban parks and feeding the wild birds that have become accustomed to humans. This activity provides people with intimate contact with urban-dwelling birds, but remember that birdseed, or better yet the birds' natural food items, are much healthier for the birds than bread and crackers.

SEASONS OF BIRDWATCHING

Spring

Spring is often the most favored season for birders, many of whom will be enthusiastically searching for early migrants at the first sign of warm weather. Each spring, Chicago is treated to a spectacular migration display as nearby rivers, valleys and shorelines funnel birds along their migration routes. By early March, large congregations of waterfowl are settling on open bodies of water, including Lake Michigan. As waterfowl numbers begin to decline, egrets and herons slowly move into the area, and by late April and early May, many of them have already settled into the cattails of local lakes and marshes, such as McGinnis Slough and McKee Marsh. Throughout late April and May, shorebirds pass through the area, followed closely by the long-anticipated landbird migration. For three weeks in May, local tracts of deciduous woodland are teeming with the bright and colorful movements of flycatchers, thrushes, vireos, warblers and sparrows. By the end of the month, however, many birds have departed for their northern breeding grounds or have already settled in their respective territories.

Summer

The Chicago area boasts an impressive list of breeding birds, and although the pace of avian life slows down during the summer months, there is still considerable activity. Many woodpeckers, including the Red-headed, Red-bellied,

Downy and Hairy, nest in and around the Chicago area, excavating cavities in old or decaying deciduous trees. Various parks host breeding raptors, such as the American Kestrel and the Eastern Screech-Owl, which choose to nest in woodland cavities, especially abandoned woodpecker holes. The lush canopies of woodland parks are popular nesting locations for many warblers and other songbirds. Some birds, such as the Warbling Vireo and the Scarlet Tanager, nest high in the treetops, but others, such as the Oven-bird, always build their nests among the leafy undergrowth of the forest bottom. Chicago's waterfront is also a great place to view water-birds during the warmer months.

Fall

The fall migrations, beginning as early as July and extending into December, are less concentrated than in spring, but they last much longer. Shorebirds are the first to travel south through our area, followed closely by flights of landbirds, most in their dull fall plumage. Landbird migration begins in late August and lasts into October and November. Fall is the time to watch great numbers of hawks passing over-head on their way south. A favorite hawk-watching locale is along the western shore of Lake Michigan at Illinois Beach State Park. In October, waterfowl concentrations are at their peak, and numbers in the thousands are not unheard-of. During fall, many of the ducks, shorebirds, gulls and warblers have acquired frustratingly similar plumages, but this season has its own benefits: the prolonged migratory season provides a much longer time for observing all sorts of interesting birds.

Winter

The winter months are a good time to find a variety of waterbirds along Chicago's lakefront. Many areas that do not freeze over attract Canada Geese, American Black Ducks, Oldsquaws, Common Mergansers and a variety of gulls, among others. A visit to any woodland park will most often reward the birder with views of many common wintering and year-round species, such as the Black-capped Chickadee, the Northern Cardinal, the American Goldfinch and, dur-ing the most mild winters, the Song Sparrow. Wood-lands are also home to resident species of woodpeckers and owls, many of which inhabit cavities in old trees and snags. Red-bellied and Downy woodpeckers are found year-round in forested areas of the Chicago region, and owls, such as the Great Horned Owl and Eastern Screech-Owl, are often more conspicuous during the winter months. Winter is also the time for birdfeeders, and a good day might attract a wide diversity of species to backyards or neighborhoods.

BIRDING OPTICS

Most people who are interested in birdwatching will eventually buy a pair of binoculars. They help you identify key bird characteristics, such as plumage and bill color, and they also help you identify other birders! Birdwatchers are a friendly sort, and a chat among birders is all part of the experience.

You'll use your binoculars often, so select a pair that will contribute to the quality of your birdwatching experience—they don't have to be expensive. If you need help deciding which pair is right for you, talk to other birdwatchers or to someone at your local nature center.

One of the first things you'll notice about binoculars (apart from the price extremes) is that they all have two numbers associated with them (8x40, for example). The first number, which is always the smallest, is the magnification (how large the bird will appear), while the second is the size (in millimeters) of the objective lens (the larger end). It might seem important at first to get the highest magnification possible, but a reasonable magnification of 7x to 8x is optimal for all-purpose birding: it draws you fairly close to most birds without causing too much shaking. Some shaking happens to everyone; to overcome it, rest the binoculars against a support, such as a partner's shoulder or a tree.

The size of the objective lens is really a question of birding conditions and weight. Because wider lenses (40–50 mm) will bring in more light, these are preferred for birding in low-light situations (like before sunrise or after sunset). If these aren't the conditions that you will be pursuing, a light pair that has an objective lens diameter of less than 30 mm might be the right choice. Because binoculars tend to become heavy after hanging around your neck all day, the compact models are becoming increasingly popular. If you have a pair that is heavy, you can purchase a strap that redistributes part of the weight to the shoulders and lower back.

Another valuable piece of equipment is a spotting scope. It is very useful when you are trying to sight waterfowl, shorebirds or soaring raptors, but it is really of no use if you are intent on seeing forest birds. A good spotting scope has a magnification of around 40x. It has a sturdy tripod or a window mount for the car. Be wary of non-birding telescopes, because they are designed for seeing stars, and their magnification is too great for birdwatching. One of the advantages of having a scope is that you will be able to see far-off birds. By setting up in one spot (or by not even leaving your car) you can observe faraway flocks that would be little more than specks in your binoculars.

With these simple pieces of equipment (none of which is truly essential) and this handy field guide, anyone can enjoy birds in their area. After experiencing the thrill of a couple of hard-won identifications, you will find yourself taking your binoculars on walks, drives and trips to the beach, forest and field. As rewards accumulate with experience, you may find the books and photos piling up and your trips being planned just to see birds!

BIRDING BY EAR

Sometimes, bird *listening* can be more effective than bird *watching*. The technique of birding by ear is gaining popularity, because listening for birds can be more efficient, productive and rewarding than waiting for a visual confirmation. Birds have distinctive songs that they use to resolve territorial disputes, and sound is therefore a useful way to identify species. It is particularly useful when trying to watch some of the smaller forest-dwelling birds. Their size and often indistinct plumage can make a visual search of the forest canopy frustrating. To facilitate auditory searches, catchy paraphrases are included in the descriptions of many of the birds. If the paraphrase just doesn't seem to work for you (they are often a personal thing) be creative and try to find one that fits. By spending time playing the song over in your head, fitting words to it, the voices of birds soon become as familiar as the voices of family members. Many excellent CDs and tapes are available at bookstores and wild-bird stores for the songs of the birds in your area.

BIRDFEEDERS

They're messy, they can be costly, and they're sprouting up in neighborhoods everywhere. Feeding birds has become a common pastime in residential communities all over North America. Although the concept is fairly straightforward, as with anything else involving birds, feeders can become quite elaborate.

The great advantage to feeding birds is that neighborhood chickadees, jays, juncos and finches are enticed into regular visits. Don't expect birds to arrive at your feeder as soon as you set it up; it can take weeks for a few regulars to incorporate your yard into their daily routine. As the popularity of your feeder grows, the number of visiting birds will increase and more species will arrive. You will notice that your feeder is busier during winter, when natural foods are less abundant. You can increase the odds of a good avian turnout by using a variety of feeders and seeds. When a number of birds habitually visit your yard, maintaining the feeder becomes a responsibility, because the birds might rely on it as a regular food source.

Larger birds tend to enjoy feeding on platforms or on the ground; smaller birds are comfortable on hanging seed dispensers. Certain seeds tend to attract specific birds; nature centers and wild-bird supply stores are the best places to ask how to attract a favorite species. It's mainly seed eaters that are attracted to backyards; some birds have no interest in feeders. Only the most committed birdwatcher will try to attract birds that are insect eaters, berry eaters or, in some extreme cases, scavengers!

The location of the feeder can influence the amount of business it receives from the neighborhood birds. Because birds are wild, they are instinctively wary, and they are unlikely to visit an area where they might come under attack. When putting up your feeder, think like a bird. A good, clear view with convenient escape routes is always appreciated. Cats like birdfeeders that are close to the ground and within pouncing distance from a bush; obviously, birds don't. Above all, a birdfeeder should be in view of a favorite window, where you can sit and enjoy the rewarding interaction of your appreciative feathered guests.

CHICAGO-AREA BIRD SOCIETIES

There are many bird societies and clubs you can join in the Chicago area. We have listed some of the larger ones here:

Chicago Audubon Society
5801-C North Pulaski Road
Chicago, IL 60646-6057
phone: (773) 539-6793
e-mail: chicago_audubon@juno.com

Illinois Audubon Society
425 B North Gilbert
Danville, IL 61834
phone: (217) 446-5085

Chicago Ornithological Society
c/o Geoff Williamson, President
4016 N. Clarendon Ave., #3N
Chicago, IL 60613
phone: (773) 935-8439

Illinois Ornithological Society
P.O. Box 1971
Evanston, IL 60204-1971
website: http://www.chias.org/ios/

Evanston North Shore Bird Club
P.O. Box 1313
Evanston, IL 60204

Du Page Birding Club
c/o Nagendra Kolluru
4308 Nutmeg Lane, #244
Lisle, IL 60532

If you want up-to-date information on birds in the Chicago area, there are two local rare bird alerts:

Chicago Area Rare Bird Alert: (847) 265-2118

Du Page County Rare Bird Alert: (630) 406-8111

Glossary

accipiter: a forest hawk (genus *Accipiter*); characterized by a long tail and short, rounded wings; feeds mostly on birds.

brood: *n.* a family of young from one hatching; *v.* sit on eggs so as to hatch them.

corvid: a member of the crow family (Corvidae); includes crows, jays, magpies and ravens.

covey: a brood or flock of partridges, quails or grouse.

crop: an enlargement of the esophagus; serves as a storage structure and (in pigeons) has glands that produce secretions.

dabbling: a foraging technique used by ducks, where the head and neck are submerged but the body and tail remain on the water's surface; dabbling ducks can usually walk easily on land, can take off without running and have brightly colored speculums.

dimorphism: the existence of two distinct forms of a species, such as between the sexes.

eclipse: the dull, female-like plumage that male ducks briefly acquire after molting from their breeding plumage.

elbow patch: a dark spot at the bend of the outstretched wing, seen from below.

flycatching: a feeding behavior where the bird leaves a perch, snatches an insect in mid-air and returns to the same perch; also known as 'hawking' or 'sallying.'

fledgling: a young chick that has just acquired its permanent flight feathers but is still dependent on its parents.

flushing: a behavior where frightened birds explode into flight in response to a disturbance.

gape: the size of the mouth opening.

irruption: a sporadic mass migration of birds into a non-breeding area.

leading edge: the front edge of the wing.

lore: the small patch between the eye and the bill.

molting: the periodic replacement of worn out feathers (often twice a year).

morphology: the science of form and shape.

nape: the back of the neck.

neotropical migrant: a bird that nests in North America but overwinters in the New World tropics.

niche: an ecological role filled by a species.

open country: a landscape that is primarily not forested.

parasitism: a relationship between two species where one benefits at the expense of the other.

phylogenetics: a method of classifying animals that puts the oldest ancestral groups before those that have arisen more recently.

pishing: making a sound to attract birds by saying *pishhh* as loudly and as wetly as possible.

polyandrous: having a mating strategy where one female breeds with several males.

polygynous: having a mating strategy where one male breeds with several females.

plucking post: a perch habitually used by an accipiter for plucking feathers from its prey.

raptor: a carnivorous (meat-eating) bird; includes eagles, hawks, falcons and owls.

rufous: rusty red in color.

speculum: a brightly colored patch in the wings of many dabbling ducks.

squeaking: making a sound to attract birds by loudly kissing the back of the hand, or by using a specially design squeaky bird call.

talons: the claws of birds of prey.

understory: the shrub or thicket layer beneath a canopy of trees.

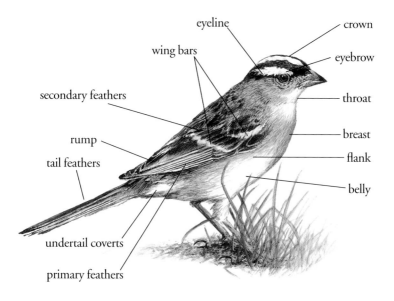

References

American Ornithologists' Union. 1983–97. *Check-list of North American Birds.* 6th ed. (and its supplements). American Ornithologists' Union, Washington, D.C.

Bohlen, H. D. 1989. *The Birds of Illinois.* Indiana University Press, Bloomington.

Chicago Audubon Society. 1998. *Birds of The Greater Chicago Area.* 2nd ed. Chicago Audubon Society, Chicago.

Ehrlich, P. R., D. S. Dobkin and D. Wheye. 1988. *The Birder's Handbook.* Fireside, New York.

Evans, H. E. 1993. *Pioneer Naturalists: The Discovery and Naming of North American Plants and Animals.* Henry Holt and Company, New York.

Farrand, J., ed. 1983. *The Audubon Society Master Guide to Birding.* 3 vols. Alfred A. Knopf, New York.

Gotch, A. F. 1981. *Birds: Their Latin Names Explained.* Blandford Press, Dorset, England.

Mearns, B., and R. Mearns. 1992. *Audubon to Xantus: The Lives of Those Commemorated in North American Bird Names.* Academic Press, San Diego.

Mlodinow, S. 1984. *Chicago Area Birds.* Chicago Review Press, Chicago.

National Audubon Society. 1971–95. *American Birds.* Vols. 25–48.

Reader's Digest Association. *Book of North American Birds.* The Reader's Digest Association, Pleasantville, New York.

Robbins, C. S., B. Brunn and H. S. Zim. 1966. *Birds of North America.* Golden Press, New York.

Scott, S. S. 1987. *Field Guide to the Birds of North America.* National Geographic Society, Washington, D.C.

Terres, J. K. 1995. *The Audubon Society Encyclopedia of North American Birds.* Wings Books, New York.

Checklist of Chicago-area Birds

The following checklist is reprinted from *Birds of the Greater Chicago Area: A Season Checklist* (1982, rev. 1998), which was compiled for the Chicago Audubon Society by Alan Richardson, Richard Biss, William DeBaets, Homer Eshbaugh, David B. Johnson, Jeffrey Sanders and Alan Stokie.

This checklist includes 313 species of birds that have been reported in the greater Chicago area since 1970. The species are listed in taxonomic order (in accordance with the 41st supplement [July 1997] of the American Ornithologists' Association's *Check-list of North American Birds*). A blank line separates each family of birds. This checklist does not include species that have been reported fewer than 10 times since 1970 and are not normally expected to be present.

For the purpose of this checklist, the 'greater Chicago area' includes

Illinois: Cook, DuPage, Grundy, Kane, Lake, McHenry and Will counties

Indiana: Lake, LaPorte and Porter counties; Willow Slough Fish and Wild life Area (Newton County); and Jasper-Pulaski State Fish and Wildlife Area (Jasper and Pulaski counties)

Wisconsin: Kenosha and Racine counties.

The checklist has been divided into six seasons to denote the differences between early and late migration periods. Note that our dates are approximate and weather dependent.

ES = Early Spring (11 March to 20 April)
LS = Late Spring (21 April to 10 June)
Su = Summer (11 June to 20 August)
EF = Early Fall (21 August to 30 September)
LF = Late Fall (1 October to 30 November)
Wi = Winter (1 December to 10 March)

Seasonal abundance:

A = Abundant (certain to be found in good numbers in several habitats)
C = Common (certain to be found in good numbers in suitable habitat)
F = Fairly Common (likely to be found in small numbers in suitable habitat)
U = Uncommon (possible to be found in small numbers in suitable habitat)
R = Rare (unlikely to be found, even in suitable habitat)
O = Occasional (one to five birds found in most years)
a = Accidental (one to five birds found in some years)

Other checklist notations:

* = Nesting (known to nest *regularly* in the area)
° = Nesting (has nested in the area, but not regularly)
l = Local (occurs only, or more commonly, in certain areas)
v = Variable (varies in presence and numbers from year to year)

	ES	LS	Su	EF	LF	Wi
Red-throated Loon	O	a	a	-	O	a
Common Loon	F	R	a	O	F	O
Pied-billed Grebe *	F	C	F	C	F	O
Horned Grebe	F	U	a	R	F	O
Red-necked Grebe	O	-	-	a	O	O
Eared Grebe °	O	O	a	O	O	a
Western Grebe	a	-	-	-	O	a
American White Pelican	O	O	O	O	O	a
Double-crested Cormorant *	F	C	C	C	C	O
American Bittern °	O	R	O	R	a	-
Least Bittern *	a	R	U	R	a	-
Great Blue Heron *	F	C	C	C	F	R
Great Egret *	U	C	C	C	U	-
Snowy Egret	-	O	O	O	a	-
Little Blue Heron	a	O	O	O	a	-
Tricolored Heron	-	a	a	a	-	-
Cattle Egret ° (l)	a	R	R	O	a	-
Green Heron *	O	F	F	U	R	a
Black-crowned Night-Heron *	U	C	C	C	R	O
Yellow-crowned Night-Heron *	a	R	R	R	a	-
Turkey Vulture *	U	U	U	U	R	a
Greater White-fronted Goose	R	a	-	a	R	O
Snow Goose	U	a	a	a	U	O
Ross's Goose	a	-	-	-	a	a
Canada Goose *	A	A	A	A	A	A
Brant	a	a	-	-	a	a
Mute Swan *	U	U	U	U	U	U
Tundra Swan	U	a	-	-	U	O
Wood Duck *	F	F	F	F	F	R
Gadwall	F	R	R	R	C	R
Eurasian Wigeon	a	a	-	-	a	a
American Wigeon	C	U	a	U	C	R
American Black Duck °	F	R	O	R	F	F
Mallard *	C	C	C	C	C	C
Blue-winged Teal *	F	F	F	C	F	a
Northern Shoveler °	F	R	U	F	O	
Northern Pintail °	R	O	O	R	U	R
Green-winged Teal	U	R	R	R	F	R
Canvasback	U	a	a	-	U	O
Redhead °	F	R	O	R	F	R
Ring-necked Duck	C	U	a	a	C	R
Greater Scaup	C	R	a	a	C	F
Lesser Scaup	C	U	a	a	C	U
King Eider	-	-	-	-	a	a
Harlequin Duck	O	a	-	-	O	O
Surf Scoter	O	O	-	a	U	O
White-winged Scoter	R	a	-	a	U	U

	ES	LS	Su	EF	LF	Wi
Black Scoter	O	a	-	a	U	O
Oldsquaw	U	a	-	-	F	F
Bufflehead	F	R	a	-	C	F
Common Goldeneye	C	O	a	a	C	C
Barrow's Goldeneye	a	-	-	-	-	a
Hooded Merganser *	U	U	R	R	F	R
Red-breasted Merganser °	C	F	O	O	C	F
Common Merganser	F	R	O	O	F	F
Ruddy Duck *	C	U	R	R	F	R
Osprey °	O	R	O	R	U	-
Bald Eagle	R	O	a	O	R	R
Northern Harrier *	U	R	R	U	F	R
Sharp-shinned Hawk °	R	R	O	F	F	O
Cooper's Hawk *	R	U	U	U	U	R
Northern Goshawk	a	a	-	a	O	O
Red-shouldered Hawk *	R	R	R	R	R	R
Broad-winged Hawk *	R	F	R	F	R	a
Swainson's Hawk * (l)	O	O	O	O	a	-
Red-tailed Hawk *	F	F	F	F	C	F
Rough-legged Hawk	U	R	a	a	U	U
Golden Eagle	a	a	a	a	O	a
American Kestrel *	U	U	U	U	U	U
Merlin	O	a	a	R	U	a
Peregrine Falcon *	R	R	R	U	R	R
Gray Partridge * (l)	O	O	O	O	O	O
Ring-necked Pheasant *	U	U	U	U	U	U
Wild Turkey (l)	O	O	O	O	O	O
Northern Bobwhite * (l)	R	R	R	R	R	R
Yellow Rail	a	a	-	a	a	-
Black Rail	a	a	a	a	-	-
King Rail °	-	O	O	O	-	a
Virginia Rail *	O	U	U	O	O	
Sora *	R	F	F	F	R	a
Common Moorhen *	a	U	U	U	O	a
American Coot *	C	C	U	C	C	R
Sandhill Crane *	C	R	R	R	C	O
Black-bellied Plover	-	U	F	F	U	a
American Golden-Plover	F	R	O	U	U	-
Semipalmated Plover	a	R	F	F	O	a
Piping Plover	a	O	O	O	a	-
Killdeer *	C	C	C	C	U	O
American Avocet	a	O	O	O	O	-
Greater Yellowlegs	U	U	U	U	U	-
Lesser Yellowlegs	U	F	C	C	U	-
Solitary Sandpiper	O	U	U	U	R	-
Willet	a	R	R	R	-	-
Spotted Sandpiper *	O	F	F	F	R	-
Upland Sandpiper * (l)	O	R	R	R	-	-

	ES	LS	Su	EF	LF	Wi
Whimbrel	-	R	O	R	-	-
Hudsonian Godwit	-	a	a	a	a	-
Marbled Godwit	-	O	O	O	a	-
Ruddy Turnstone	-	U	U	U	R	a
Red Knot	-	R	O	R	O	a
Sanderling	-	U	U	F	F	a
Semipalmated Sandpiper	a	U	C	C	U	-
Western Sandpiper	-	O	R	R	a	-
Least Sandpiper	R	U	C	C	O	a
White-rumped Sandpiper	-	U	a	R	O	-
Baird's Sandpiper	a	O	R	U	R	-
Pectoral Sandpiper	U	F	F	F	U	a
Purple Sandpiper	a	a	a	-	O	O
Dunlin	a	U	a	F	F	a
Stilt Sandpiper	-	R	U	U	-	-
Buff-breasted Sandpiper	-	-	R	R	O	-
Ruff/Reeve	a	a	a	a	-	-
Short-billed Dowitcher	a	U	F	F	R	-
Long-billed Dowitcher	-	a	O	O	R	-
Common Snipe °	U	R	R	F	U	O
American Woodcock *	U	U	U	U	R	a
Wilson's Phalarope	-	R	R	R	a	-
Red-necked Phalarope	-	a	a	a	a	-
Red Phalarope	-	-	a	a	O	a
Pomarine Jaeger	-	-	a	a	a	a
Parasitic Jaeger	-	-	-	R	R	a
Long-tailed Jaeger	-	-	a	a	a	-
Laughing Gull	a	O	O	O	O	-
Franklin's Gull	a	O	O	R	U	a
Little Gull	a	a	a	a	O	O
Black-headed Gull	a	a	a	a	a	-
Bonaparte's Gull	C	C	O	U	C	R
Mew Gull	a	-	-	-	a	O
Ring-billed Gull *	C	C	C	A	A	C
California Gull	a	-	-	a	a	a
Herring Gull *	C	C	F	C	C	C
Thayer's Gull	R	O	a	a	R	U
Iceland Gull	O	O	a	-	O	O
Lesser Black-backed Gull	O	O	a	a	O	O
Glaucous Gull	U	O	a	a	R	U
Great Black-backed Gull	R	O	a	a	O	R
Black-legged Kittiwake	a	a	-	a	R	O
Sabine's Gull	-	-	-	a	O	-
Caspian Tern °	R	U	U	F	R	-
Common Tern °	O	F	R	F	R	-
Forster's Tern °	R	U	R	F	R	-
Least Tern	-	a	a	-	-	-
Black Tern *	-	U	U	U	a	-
Rock Dove *	A	A	A	A	A	A
Mourning Dove *	F	C	C	A	C	F
Monk Parakeet * (l)	R	R	R	R	R	R
Black-billed Cuckoo *	-	U	U	R	a	-
Yellow-billed Cuckoo *	-	U	U	U	a	-
Barn Owl	a	a	-	a	a	a
Eastern Screech-Owl *	U	U	U	U	U	F
Great Horned Owl *	U	U	U	U	U	U
Snowy Owl (v)	a	-	-	-	O	R
Barred Owl * (l)	R	R	R	R	R	R
Long-eared Owl ° (v)	O	a	a	-	O	R

	ES	LS	Su	EF	LF	Wi
Short-eared Owl	U	R	a	a	U	U
Northern Saw-whet Owl	O	a	a	a	O	O
Common Nighthawk *	-	U	F	A	a	-
Chuck-will's-widow ° (l)	-	O	O	-	-	-
Whip-poor-will * (l)	O	U	U	O	a	-
Chimney Swift *	O	C	C	A	U	-
Ruby-throated Hummingbird *	O	U	U	U	O	-
Belted Kingfisher *	U	U	U	U	U	R
Red-headed Woodpecker *	U	F	F	F	U	R
Red-bellied Woodpecker *	F	F	F	F	F	F
Yellow-bellied Sapsucker	U	R	a	U	F	O
Downy Woodpecker *	F	F	F	F	F	F
Hairy Woodpecker *	U	U	U	U	U	U
Northern Flicker *	F	C	F	C	F	R
Pileated Woodpecker °	O	O	O	O	O	O
Olive-sided Flycatcher	-	R	O	R	a	-
Eastern Wood-Pewee *	-	C	C	F	a	-
Yellow-bellied Flycatcher	-	U	O	R	-	-
Acadian Flycatcher *	-	U	U	?	-	-
Alder Flycatcher *	-	U	U	?	-	-
Willow Flycatcher *	-	F	F	?	-	-
Least Flycatcher °	a	C	U	?	-	-
Eastern Phoebe *	F	U	U	U	F	O
Great Crested Flycatcher *	-	F	F	U	a	-
Western Kingbird °	-	a	a	a	a	-
Eastern Kingbird *	-	C	C	U	-	a
Northern Shrike	O	a	-	-	O	O
Loggerhead Shrike ° (l)	O	O	O	O	-	-
White-eyed Vireo * (l)	a	R	R	O	a	a
Bell's Vireo * (l)	-	R	R	O	a	-
Blue-headed Vireo	a	R	a	R	-	-
Yellow-throated Vireo *	a	U	U	R	a	-
Warbling Vireo *	-	C	C	F	a	-
Philadelphia Vireo	-	U	a	U	O	-
Red-eyed Vireo *	a	C	C	F	O	-
Blue Jay *	F	C	F	F	F	F
American Crow *	A	A	A	A	A	A
Horned Lark *	F	U	U	U	F	F
Purple Martin *	R	F	F	C	a	-
Tree Swallow *	F	F	F	F	R	a
Northern Rough-winged Swallow *	O	F	U	R	a	-
Bank Swallow *	O	F	U	R	a	-
Barn Swallow *	U	C	C	C	R	-
Cliff Swallow *	a	U	U	U	-	-
Black-capped Chickadee *	C	C	C	C	C	C
Tufted Titmouse * (l)	U	U	U	U	U	U
Red-breasted Nuthatch ° (v)	U	R	a	U	F	R
White-breasted Nuthatch *	F	F	F	F	F	F
Brown Creeper °	F	R	a	U	F	R

	ES	LS	Su	EF	LF	Wi
❏ Carolina Wren * (l)	R	R	R	R	R	R
❏ House Wren *	a	C	C	U	a	a
❏ Winter Wren	U	R	a	R	F	O
❏ Sedge Wren *	O	U	U	R	O	-
❏ Marsh Wren *	R	F	F	U	R	a
❏ Golden-crowned Kinglet °	F	O	a	O	F	R
❏ Ruby-crowned Kinglet	U	F	-	U	F	a
❏ Blue-gray Gnatcatcher *	R	U	U	R	-	-
❏ Eastern Bluebird *	U	U	U	U	U	O
❏ Veery *	O	F	U	U	O	-
❏ Gray-cheeked Thrush	a	U	a	U	O	a
❏ Swainson's Thrush	a	C	a	C	O	a
❏ Hermit Thrush	F	F	a	F	F	R
❏ Wood Thrush *	a	F	F	U	a	-
❏ American Robin *	C	A	A	A	C	U
❏ Varied Thrush	a	a	-	-	a	a
❏ European Starling *	A	A	A	A	A	A
❏ Gray Catbird *	a	C	C	C	U	a
❏ Northern Mockingbird * (l)	O	R	O	a	a	a
❏ Brown Thrasher *	R	F	F	U	R	a
❏ American Pipit	O	R	-	O	R	-
❏ Bohemian Waxwing	a	a	-	-	a	a
❏ Cedar Waxwing *	F	F	F	C	F	F
❏ Blue-winged Warbler *	a	F	F	U	-	-
❏ Golden-winged Warbler *	-	U	R	U	-	-
❏ Tennessee Warbler	a	C	O	C	O	-
❏ Orange-crowned Warbler	O	U	a	R	R	a
❏ Nashville Warbler *	O	C	a	C	R	a
❏ Northern Parula *	a	U	a	R	a	a
❏ Yellow Warbler *	a	C	C	F	O	a
❏ Chestnut-sided Warbler °	a	C	R	F	O	-
❏ Magnolia Warbler	O	C	a	C	R	a
❏ Cape May Warbler	-	U	a	U	O	a
❏ Black-throated Blue Warbler	-	R	a	R	a	-
❏ Yellow-rumped Warbler	U	A	a	C	C	R
❏ Black-throated Green Warbler °	a	C	O	C	R	-
❏ Blackburnian Warbler	-	U	O	U	a	-
❏ Yellow-throated Warbler °	a	O	a	-	-	a
❏ Pine Warbler	O	R	-	R	O	a
❏ Prairie Warbler ° (l)	a	R	R	R	-	-
❏ Palm Warbler	O	C	a	C	F	a
❏ Bay-breasted Warbler	a	C	a	C	R	-
❏ Blackpoll Warbler	a	C	a	C	O	-
❏ Cerulean Warbler * (l)	-	U	U	O	a	-
❏ Black-and-white Warbler °	O	F	O	F	R	a
❏ American Redstart *	a	C	U	C	U	a
❏ Prothonotory Warbler * (l)	a	R	R	R	-	a
❏ Worm-eating Warbler	a	O	a	a	-	-
❏ Ovenbird *	a	F	U	U	O	a
❏ Northern Waterthrush	O	F	a	F	R	a
❏ Louisiana Waterthrush *	R	R	R	O	-	-
❏ Kentucky Warbler * (l)	a	O	O	a	-	-
❏ Connecticut Warbler	-	R	a	R	a	-
❏ Mourning Warbler °	-	U	R	R	a	-
❏ Common Yellowthroat *	O	C	C	F	R	a
❏ Hooded Warbler * (l)	a	R	R	O	a	-
❏ Wilson's Warbler	-	F	a	F	a	a

	ES	LS	Su	EF	LF	Wi
❏ Canada Warbler °	-	U	O	R	-	-
❏ Yellow-breasted Chat *	-	U	U	O	-	a
❏ Summer Tanager °	a	O	O	-	-	-
❏ Scarlet Tanager *	-	F	F	R	a	-
❏ Western Tanager	-	a	-	-	-	-
❏ Eastern Towhee *	U	F	F	U	R	O
❏ Spotted Towhee	-	a	-	-	a	a
❏ American Tree Sparrow	C	R	-	a	F	C
❏ Chipping Sparrow *	R	F	F	F	U	a
❏ Clay-colored Sparrow °	a	R	a	R	O	a
❏ Field Sparrow *	R	C	C	F	F	R
❏ Vesper Sparrow *	R	U	U	U	R	a
❏ Lark Sparrow * (l)	a	R	R	O	a	-
❏ Lark Bunting	a	a	-	a	-	a
❏ Savannah Sparrow *	F	C	C	F	U	a
❏ Grasshopper Sparrow *	a	U	U	R	a	-
❏ Henslow's Sparrow * (l)	a	R	R	O	a	-
❏ Le Conte's Sparrow	O	R	-	R	R	a
❏ Nelson's Sharp-tailed Sparrow	a	R	-	R	R	-
❏ Fox Sparrow	F	R	-	O	U	R
❏ Song Sparrow *	C	C	C	C	C	F
❏ Lincoln's Sparrow	O	U	a	U	U	a
❏ Swamp Sparrow *	U	F	U	F	F	R
❏ White-throated Sparrow	U	C	O	U	C	U
❏ Harris's Sparrow	a	O	a	a	O	a
❏ White-crowned Sparrow	O	F	a	R	F	R
❏ Dark-eyed Junco	C	R	a	U	A	A
❏ Lapland Longspur	U	O	-	a	U	U
❏ Smith's Longspur (l)	O	-	-	a	a	-
❏ Snow Bunting	U	a	-	-	U	F
❏ Northern Cardinal *	A	A	A	A	A	A
❏ Rose-breasted Grosbeak *	a	F	F	F	R	a
❏ Blue Grosbeak ° (l)	-	O	O	-	-	-
❏ Indigo Bunting *	a	C	C	R	a	a
❏ Dickcissel *	-	U	U	O	a	a
❏ Bobolink *	-	F	F	U	a	-
❏ Red-winged Blackbird *	C	A	A	A	A	R
❏ Eastern Meadowlark *	U	F	F	F	U	R
❏ Western Meadowlark *	R	R	R	R	a	-
❏ Yellow-headed Blackbird *	R	U	U	R	a	a
❏ Rusty Blackbird	U	R	-	R	F	O
❏ Brewer's Blackbird	O	O	O	O	O	a
❏ Common Grackle *	A	A	A	A	A	R
❏ Brown-headed Cowbird *	F	C	C	U	C	R
❏ Baltimore Oriole *	a	F	F	U	O	a
❏ Orchard Oriole * (l)	-	U	U	O	-	-
❏ Pine Grosbeak (v)	a	-	-	a	a	a
❏ Purple Finch	U	U	a	R	U	U
❏ House Finch *	C	C	C	C	C	F
❏ Red Crossbill ° (v)	U	a	a	a	U	U
❏ White-winged Crossbill (v)	O	a	-	-	a	O
❏ Common Redpoll (v)	R	a	-	-	R	U
❏ Hoary Redpoll	a	-	-	-	a	a
❏ Pine Siskin °	U	R	a	a	U	U
❏ American Goldfinch *	F	F	C	C	C	F
❏ Evening Grosbeak (v)	R	a	-	a	R	R
❏ House Sparrow *	A	A	A	A	A	A

Index of Scientific Names

This index references only the primary, illustrated species descriptions.

Index of Common Names

Numbers in boldface type refer to illustrated species descriptions.

About the Authors

When he's not out watching birds, frogs or snakes, Chris Fisher researches endangered species management and wildlife interpretation at the University of Alberta in Edmonton. The appeal of wildlife and wilderness has led him on many travels, including frequent visits with birds, throughout North America and as far away as Thailand. By sharing his enthusiasm and passion for wild things through lectures, photographs and articles, Chris strives to foster a greater appreciation for the value of our wilderness.

David Johnson brings to this project more than 25 years of birding experience in the Chicago area. He is an avid birder, tour leader and writer, and he is currently an associate editor of the *Meadowlark*, a journal of Illinois birds published by the Illinois Ornithological Society. David is heavily involved in the local birding community, leading field trips and organizing and participating in many breeding bird surveys and Christmas and spring bird counts. He is a member of nine local, regional and national birding associations. In 1996, the Chicago Audubon Society named David a Protector of the Environment, and in 1998 it awarded him a Silver Anniversary honor for long-term service to the birds and birders of Chicagoland.

PRACTICAL
GARDEN STONEWORK

PRACTICAL
GARDEN
STONEWORK

by Geoff Hamilton

London.
W. FOULSHAM & CO. LTD
New York · Toronto · Capetown · Sydney

W. FOULSHAM & COMPANY LIMITED
Yeovil Road, SLOUGH, Berkshire SL1 4JH

ISBN 0-572-01642-5
© W. Foulsham & Co. Ltd. 1991
Originally published as
Do Your Own Garden Stonework
All Rights Reserved.

Designed by Stonecastle Graphics

Photographs facing pages 32 and 33 are by courtesy of
S. MARSHALL & SONS LTD of HALIFAX
Photographs facing pages 64 and 65 are by courtesy of the
CEMENT & CONCRETE ASSOCIATION

Printed and bound in Great Britain
at The Bath Press, Avon

Contents

Gardens are there to be used, so they need a paved area for sitting out in all seasons and enjoying the fresh air.

Introduction

Throughout civilized man's history, stone, brick or concrete have been essential to his way of life. And, though some of the materials may have changed over the years, and building techniques have developed, we rely as much on them today as ever we did. Indeed, more so. Perhaps the day may come when metal and plastics take the place of more traditional materials, but that day is certainly not in the foreseeable future.

There must be very few gardens that do not sport a concrete driveway, a paved path or a patio for sitting out and enjoying the fresh air. Gardens are there to be *used*, not just in the summer, but also for that near half-year when our climate makes grass and soil inhospitable.

So most gardens will need a hard-standing for the car, a dry path alongside the washing line or a paved area where one can sit in the sunshine, eat out on warmer days or entertain one's friends to a barbecue.

As the need for housing becomes more acute, gardens are getting smaller, and sites more scarce. This inevitably results in 'difficult' gardens, where perhaps the land slopes sharply away from or towards the house. Then, the only solution is to build retaining walls and steps, and to landscape the garden into a series of flat, usable terraces. Properly done, this sort of garden can become a far more interesting and attractive feature than one built entirely on the flat.

In completely flat gardens, some sort of feature may be required to add height to an otherwise uninteresting vista. A raised bed, a brick flower-box or even a stone seat can make just that feature that makes all the difference.

This book sets out to provide the basic information necessary for the 'do-it-yourselfer' to tackle his own patio, driveway, retaining wall, or indeed any stonework project with the exception of pools and rock gardens. That's a subject for a book on its own.

To the gardener just starting from scratch, all this 'hard' landscaping may seem a daunting proposition. All that concrete to mix, and those heavy slabs to hump about. Well, in all honesty, it *is* going to be hard work. There are not many short cuts and, unless you do the job properly, you are wasting your time. But, once you get into it, I can almost guarantee that you'll find it an absorbing and highly satisfying job. A chance to create a thing of beauty that you'll be able to enjoy for the rest of your life. Because, done properly, a stone patio, a brick wall or a concrete driveway *will* last a lifetime. And it will add more than its cost to the value of your house.

1 Planning

Before you dig out a shovelful of soil or mix a barrowload of concrete, give your new project long and serious thought. Bear in mind that your handiwork will be there for a long, long time. You *must* get it right first time.

Start by taking a few walks around your new 'estate' to get the feel of the place. Make sure you know which parts of the garden are likely to be in full sun and which will be shaded for part of the day. If you are building a patio, for example, decide what times of the day you are most likely to use it, and ensure that at those times it will be bathed in sunshine if you are a sun-lover, or that it will be in the shade if you find the heat oppressive.

Think about the garden as a whole. It is no good, for instance, siting the washing line in a spot where the clean sheets will flap all over the roses. That does neither of them any good. Don't build that decorative wall to mask the dustbins to the windward of your sitting-out area, and don't hide the coal-bunker at the far end of the garden where you'll freeze to death fetching the coal on a wintry night.

Above all, discuss your ideas in depth with your wife or your husband. Two heads are always better than one.

When you really feel that you know the site, it's time to start committing a few ideas to paper. Again, there is no rush. You almost certainly won't get it right first time.

Measure up the rough size and shape of the plot, and draw it out on a sheet of paper. There is no need at this stage to be too accurate. Start by drawing in the essentials. Certainly you'll want a hard path leading to both front and rear doors, you may need a hard-standing for the car, and this can generally only be put in one place, and most families will need somewhere to dry the washing. You should consider a spot for the dustbin, and you may need to provide a path to the rear gate.

Even with these factors, there is room for manoeuvre and a chance to make an attractive feature. A brick path winding round the edge of the lawn, for instance, will look attractive, fulfil a useful function, and make the maintenance of the grass much easier too. Even the place where the rubbish is left for the dustman can be made to look attractive by hiding it with a decorative wall, perhaps covered with roses or sweet-smelling honeysuckle. You'll soon begin to realize that this is one of the most exciting stages of the whole operation.

If you are building paths or walls across the garden, try not to cut it into strips. This will only serve to reduce the apparent size of the garden. Often, by building in some curves, you can actually make the garden seem to increase in size.

1. By building some curves into the garden, it can be made to look larger than it really is.

2. A corner patio is often more useful than the conventional long, thin strip at the back of the house.

Of course, at this stage you will also have to take some account of cost. But don't let the thought of your bank manager's apoplexy prevent you from *planning* your project, even if you can't afford it all at once. If the job is properly planned, there is no reason at all why you should not complete it in stages. But it should be planned as a whole at the outset. There is nothing worse than the garden which is planned piecemeal. It will always look as though half of it has been an afterthought, and will never come together as a cohesive entity.

As well as thinking about the aesthetic appeal of a feature, you should also consider its usefulness. If, for example, you wish to build a patio, make sure that it is made to a usable shape. The long thin strip outside the back of the house, so beloved of all builders apparently, is virtually useless. Try putting a table and half-a-dozen chairs round it for an alfresco meal, and the poor chap nearest the edge will be in constant danger of falling off! Using exactly the same amount of paving, the patio could be built at one end of the house in a square, triangular or semicircular shape, to provide a much more accessible area.

But, even if the bank balance is becoming stretched, beware of skimping. That is the greatest folly of them all. Narrow paths always look mean and ugly and, though it may seem a paradox, make the whole garden shrink. There is no real rule of thumb for determining size, except that the separate features should be in scale with the rest of the garden.

Every garden should be a green and pleasant place, and however hard you try, 'hard' landscaping will tend to look unnatural. So allow plenty of scope for softening it with plants. A large area of paving can be broken up and 'softened' by leaving areas in it unpaved to grow plants. Just by cutting off the corner of a slab, filling the hole with soil and planting an alpine plant or a prostrate conifer, you will add interest and colour. And the patio will start to become an integral part of the garden scheme rather than standing out like a sore thumb.

3. Leave some spaces so that 'hard' areas of paving can be softened by judicious planting.

Similar holes can be left in walls, so that a few plants can be poked in to soften the hard lines. If you need to build double walls, the top can be left unfilled, so that it can be planted and brought to life.

It is essential, too, at the planning stage to think about levels, and this is particularly so if the garden is on a slope.

If the patio is to be sited next to the house wall, it *must* finish at least two courses below the damp-proof course. Failure to do this will result in water creeping through the wall to the inside of the house, and destroying plaster and wallpaper. A daunting thought indeed.

It must also slope away from the house so that rain water runs away from the wall. This may mean that a retaining wall may need to be built at the edge of the patio, and this must be planned at the outset.

You may also have to think about drainage, especially if the garden slopes towards the house. If the patio is

4. Wide paths can also be planted to 'soften' the hard lines while still retaining their usefulness.

enclosed with a retaining wall, there will be nowhere for the water to get away. And after a heavy storm, there could be a lot of water on a large area of paving. Naturally, the drains must be built before the paving is laid, so they too must be planned right from the start.

With all these factors to be borne in mind, even the best of planners take a long time and make dozens of rough drawings. It is well worth it in the end.

Finally, bear in mind that a garden is an intensely personal thing. It is a living manifestation of your own ideas and your own personality. No-one can advise you on that. If it suits *you*, then it is right. You cannot get that sort of inspiration from other people or from a book. Not even this one.

2 Choosing

With so many different types of paving and walling available, the prospective buyer is often faced with a knotty problem. Of course, price will make a big difference, but this should not, if at all possible, be allowed to dominate your choice. It is generally better to settle for nothing less than the best material for the job, even if it means either delaying the work for a while, or completing it in stages. Remember that the feature will be there for life, and the cost will certainly be recouped if the house is sold. Above all, you have to live with it and *enjoy* it, so the first criterion should be to choose a material that is pleasing to your eye.

There are other more practical considerations to be borne in mind too. If, for example, your proposed patio is in a situation or of a design that will entail a lot of cutting of slabs, it is important to buy paving that will cut easily and cheaply with a chisel. The hire of a stone saw for more difficult slabs will increase the cost of the job considerably.

If you are laying a path that is to be continually in the shade, moss and algae will almost certainly form on the surface, making it very slippery. This can be very dangerous indeed, especially to visitors, who may be unaware of the conditions. In this case, slabs with a non-slip surface are absolutely essential if nasty accidents are to be avoided.

The size of slabs may be an important consideration too. If, for example, you intend to pave a path 1m(3ft) wide, it would be quite impracticable to buy slabs 60cm(2ft) wide. That would mean that every other slab would have to be cut in half. A time-consuming and unrewarding job.

The thickness of the slabs you buy must also be taken

into account. If you intend to run the car over them, let alone the tanker that fills the oil storage tank, they *must* be no less than 5cm(2in) thick. Anything thinner will almost certainly crack under the weight of a vehicle. In this case, insist on slabs that have been machine pressed as opposed to those that have been moulded. Pressed slabs are much stronger.

If you are simply building a patio or a path that will be used only for pedestrian traffic, your choice is much wider. Here, thinner slabs are quite satisfactory, and much lighter. This means that, provided you choose slabs of a reasonable size, you will be able to handle them yourself and will not have to rely on help from friends or neighbours. Generally speaking, a fit, able-bodied man not plagued with back troubles should be able to handle slabs 60cm × 60cm × 5cm (2ft × 2ft × 2in) all day without too much problem. If you're not used to that sort of work, take it easy and don't try to do too much at once. That may be difficult, because once you start, you'll certainly want to carry on. But, the following morning, you'll know you've done it!

Bricks, must be chosen with a view to the job they have to do. First *never* use common fletton bricks in the garden, they are made for inside walls and will flake right from the very first frost.

Sand-faced flettons or stock bricks can be used in the garden for walling, but they should not be used for brick paving. They are made for situations where water will run off them immediately – in other words, for walls. If water lies on them during freezing weather, the surfaces will flake very quickly. And they then look very unattractive indeed. For paving, use engineering bricks, which are very tough and will withstand any amount of frost.

Types of paving

Materials. Basically, there are three types of paving available – natural stone, reconstituted stone and concrete. Natural stone is generally considered to be the 'crème de la crème' of materials, especially if it is to be used around an

16

older property. It has two disadvantages. It is becoming very hard to come by, especially if you are looking for second-hand stone, but it is also extremely expensive. Often the cost lies in transport, so if you are lucky enough to live near a local source it may be a little cheaper. Most natural stone will cut easily with a chisel.

Reconstituted natural stone is an acceptable alternative. The only difference between this and concrete is that, instead of using flint ballast in the concrete, natural stone chippings and dust are used. This gives the stone a much 'softer' appearance, and makes it easier to cut by hand.

Concrete is so well known that it needs no description. It is generally cheaper than natural or reconstituted stone but it is difficult, if not impossible, to cut by hand. So the cost of hiring a stone saw must be taken into account. Some concrete slabs are coloured, and it should be remembered that the colours will almost certainly fade after a period of exposure to the elements.

Colour. Paving slabs are obtainable in a wide variety of colours, some of them initially quite vivid. Generally, highly coloured paving, unless perhaps you live in the south of France or in Bermuda, is difficult to live with. It is certainly not restful to the eye, and it is very difficult to select plants that will live happily with the bright colours. Perhaps the one exception is around the swimming pool.

Try to choose a colour that will match its surroundings. If, for example, you live in a stone cottage, it would be the height of folly to choose light grey, concrete slabs. They will always stand out like a sore thumb. In this case, if you can't afford the same natural stone, choose a colour and texture as near to the stone of the house as possible.

Naturally, brick walls in the garden are best chosen to match the walls of the house. If this is impossible, and the garden walls are to be built in close proximity to the house, it may be safer to choose a completely different brick, rather than finishing up with a 'near miss'.

Shape. Undoubtedly the most popular type of paving is rectangular. It can be bought in various sizes, so it is possible to make attractive 'random' patterns. For paving around a house, or in the garden, this is much to be desired. Square paving set in straight lines gives a much harder, 'municipal' effect, though it can be used to good effect where a strictly formal scheme is envisaged.

Hexagonal slabs tend, in my opinion, to look rather 'fussy', but are useful in large areas of rectangular paving to create a change in texture. It is also possible to buy 'fish-shaped' tiles, which slot together; these can look attractive in small areas but are time-consuming to lay.

Crazy paving is in a class of its own. The Victorians are to blame for the acres of crazy paving around even modern houses, where it is quite out of place. They have a lot to answer for. Crazy paving has a place in the garden of an old country cottage, but that's about all. It does *not* fit in with modern architecture at all. It has the one dubious advantage that it is possible to buy it very cheaply from the local authority yard. Here, damaged slabs that have been removed from pavements are stored, and they are often only too pleased to see the back of them. You may have to arrange your own transport though.

1. Undoubtedly, rectangular paving is the most popular choice for the do-it-yourselfer.

2. Crazy paving can look fine in the garden of an old house but can be out of place in newer gardens.

Surface finish. Slabs are available in a variety of finishes, from the very smooth, concrete pavings to those finished by exposing the aggregate to form a very rough surface.

Choice is very much a personal matter, but certain practical applications should be considered. Round the swimming pool, it is logical to choose the smoothest surface possible, for comfort when lying in the sun. As has already been mentioned, in shady areas where slabs are likely to become slippery, a non-slip surface is best.

Some pavings are made with a 'riven' finish to match the appearance of natural stone when it wears. Often these slabs can look very attractive and are an excellent alternative to natural stone.

It is also possible to buy pavings with a moulded surface made to represent another material entirely. Stable blocks can now be obtained in a slab, while others look very much like brick paving. These slabs tend to be quite expensive, but not nearly so costly as the real thing. Naturally, they are very much easier to lay.

3. Coloured paving tends to be a little garish, though it can be effective round a swimming pool.

Ordering

If you are laying slabs of one size, or if you use crazy paving, ordering is simple. Simply measure up the area, allow a couple of square metres for breakages, and order in square metres. But if you intend to use a random rectangular pattern, ordering is a little more complicated. There are two alternatives. You can draw out the area to scale and work out a pattern before you start. This way you can order just the number and sizes of slabs you need.

Altenatively you may prefer to work out the pattern as you lay the slabs, thus giving an entirely informal effect. In this case it will be impossible to work out in advance the exact number of each size you will need. The best method is to measure out the total area and divide it by the number of different sizes you intend to use. Then ask the merchant to deliver equal *areas* (not numbers) of each size. When you get near the end, you will be able to see more accurately what you need to finish the job. You should only need a few slabs, which can perhaps be picked up from the merchant by car, to avoid the additional cost of delivery.

3 Tools

Before starting on the work, make sure that you have all the tools you need. You will always discover that you have forgotten to buy the spirit level on a Sunday afternoon when the builder's merchant is closed. And more often than not, you will have just mixed a large batch of mortar that you won't be able to use. That's the Law of the Cussedness of Nature and should be guarded against.

Some tools you will be able to make yourself, but many will have to be bought. With a few exceptions, it is best to buy top-quality tools and to look after them. Many of them will be used in the garden or around the house later, so it will be money well spent.

Wheelbarrow

A good barrow will save a great deal of effort. There are many very pretty models on the market, but there is still nothing to beat the good, old-fashioned navvy-barrow. They are made for hard work and lots of it, and should last you a lifetime. Choose one with a pneumatic tyre. They are much easier to push when they are loaded, especially if the ground is rough.

Spade, fork and shovel

These basic gardening tools will be used time and time again in the garden. So again it is worth buying the best. If you can afford it buy a stainless-steel spade because they make the digging out a positive pleasure. For the fork and shovel ordinary forged steel is quite good enough. Don't be over-ambitious, especially with the shovel. Choose one you can comfortably work with all day.

Straightedge

It sounds obvious but it really is very important to make sure that your straightedge is straight. A lump of twisted softwood will be worse than useless, and your paving, walling or concrete will finish up all over the place.

Buy a piece of hardwood about 7.5cm × 2.5cm × 3m (3in × 1in × 10ft) and get the timber merchant to plane it straight on his planer. Then, just to make sure, hold it up to your eye, and sight down it. Any twists or deviations will easily be seen.

Trowels

For paving and walling, you will need two trowels. Again, buy the best. For handling mortar for both jobs, you'll need a large, bricklayer's trowel, and for pointing afterwards, a smaller pointing trowel is required.

Spirit level

Spirit levels are not cheap, so if you are unlikely to use them after the stonework job is completed, try to borrow from a friend, or even hire from a small tool agency. Ideally, you should have a small level, about 23cm(9in) long for working in restricted areas, and a 1m(3ft) level for general paving and walling work. If the worst comes to the worst, you can use the small level on top of the straightedge for levelling paving, but it is nothing like as convenient.

Club hammer

A 1.5kg(3lb) club hammer will be necessary for laying paving, and for cutting slabs and bricks. If you are doing a lot of paving, you'll ruin the handle, so an expensive hammer is a luxury.

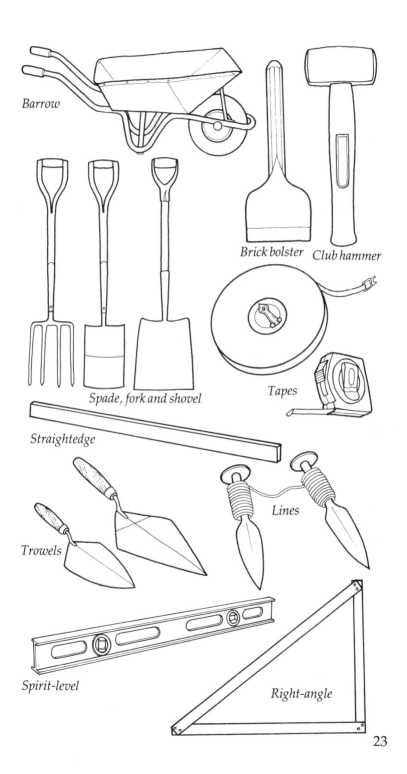

Barrow

Brick bolster   Club hammer

Spade, fork and shovel

Tapes

Straightedge

Trowels

Lines

Spirit-level

Right-angle

23

You may, in fact, find that a hammer of this weight is a little clumsy to use. In this case, handle the hammer before buying and, if it feels too heavy, settle for a lighter one.

Bolsters

Ideally, you should buy a stone bolster and a brick bolster. But the heavier stone bolsters are rather difficult to obtain, so you may have to make do with a brick bolster for both jobs. With a little practice, it will do a perfectly good job of cutting stone. Again, since neither is likely to be used a lot after the stonework is done, you may prefer to borrow or hire.

Tapes

Measuring tapes are essential for many jobs in the new garden. It really is important to measure up accurately before committing your garden design to paper, and you'll need them again during the actual work. For measuring larger areas use a surveyor's tape, and for closer work you'll also need a good steel tape. Don't make do with your wife's dressmaking tape-measure or your son's school ruler. Slabs and bricks are made to accurate and uniform measurements so you will need to be accurate too.

Lines

For surveying, you will need a good garden line, and you will also find a bricklayer's line, which is thinner, invaluable. Make sure they are made of nylon, since this won't stretch. Brickies generally use special pins for holding their lines, but I have found a couple of large nails to be adequate.

Spot-board

When you are laying bricks, or pointing, you will find it much easier if the mortar is placed on a board. Builders call them 'spot-boards', but they are nothing more or less than a lump of wood about 1m × 1m(3ft × 3ft). You should be able to find a suitable piece knocking around behind the shed.

Right-angle

For surveying you will almost certainly need to measure a right-angle. For short measurements, use a carpenter's square, or preferably a roofing square. For measuring on a larger scale you can make a right-angle out of wood. Simply measure three lengths of scrap wood to form a 3,4,5 triangle, and nail them together. The angle between the two shortest sides will be a right-angle.

Bucket

You will certainly need a good, large, strong bucket for carrying water. Buy one of the strong, plastic variety from the builder's merchant. It will get plenty of use later.

Broom

One of the most useful tools of the trade, the broom should be in constant use. If you sweep up regularly, and keep the job clean at all times, the finished result will be much, much better. You'll need a stiff, yard broom for cleaning down the driveway after mixing concrete, and a soft broom for cleaning the slabs and brickwork.

Tools to hire

If you have a lot of concreting to do, you will find the hire of a small concrete mixer invaluable. It will save an enormous amount of time and effort and is well worth the expense.

For cutting concrete slabs, you can hire a stone saw, sometimes called an angle-grinder. This consists of a motorized abrasive wheel that will cut through almost anything. They are quite expensive to hire, and use up the discs at an alarming rate.

Maintenance

There is nothing worse than trying to work with tools that are encrusted with half a ton of hardened concrete. It is frustrating, time-consuming, and a sign of a bad workman. *Always* clean your tools in water at the end of every day's work, especially if you have borrowed or hired them. After washing them, dry them with a bit of old sacking and put them away where you'll find them straight away the following morning.

After work each day, make sure that your tools are well washed to remove all traces of cement.

4 Setting out

The importance of careful planning cannot be overstated. It really is vital to draw up a careful plan of the whole garden incorporating the patio, path or wall before starting on the job. Only in this way can the effect be visualized and the correct proportions ascertained.

Perhaps the most difficult task of the landscape gardener, even the professional, is to visualize the finished effect of any feature in the garden. The task is made very much easier if the proposed feature is first committed to paper. After that, it is well worthwhile marking out the site with pegs and string to assist the imagination.

To make drawings that are accurate enough for the purpose does not require sophisticated instruments, nor do you need to take a course in surveying. With the possible exception of a good surveyor's tape, you will almost certainly find all you need in the garage or the garden shed. A very basic understanding of simple geometry completes the necessary equipment.

Measuring up

The first essential is to measure up and draw the boundaries of the garden. If the site is exactly rectangular, this is a very simple matter. But, in my experience, gardens rarely are.

So you must start by finding two objects that are fixed. The easiest way is to use the two corners of the house.

Equip yourself with a clip-board, (a piece of scrap plywood and a bulldog clip), and a piece of paper. Start by drawing roughly the shape of the garden, with the house in the drawing. There is no need to be at all accurate at this stage.

Now, from each corner of the house, measure to the corners of the garden and mark the measurements on the drawing. Then measure any fixed objects, such as trees, or perhaps the clothes post or the coal bunker if you don't intend to move them, in exactly the same way. Always make two measurements from each corner of the house.

In order to be able to check your measurements later, it is as well also to measure the lengths of the boundaries. With all these measurements drawn into the rough drawings, you are now ready to start on the accurate plan.

On a large piece of paper (squared paper makes the job much easier) draw in the house. It must be drawn to scale, and this is normally something like 5cm to 1m or, if you prefer to work in feet and inches, about 2in to 1yd.

Now, using a pair of compasses, draw an arc from one corner of the house to the first corner of the garden as measured on your rough plan. Repeat this exercise from the other corner, so that the two arcs cross. Where they cross is the corner of the garden.

Repeat this for the second corner, and draw a line joining the two. Confirm now that your measurements are correct by working out the distance between the two corners and checking the measurement you made on the rough plan. Do the same to establish all the points you measured and you have an accurate, scale drawing of the garden.

Make this drawing your 'master-plan'. Ink it in if you feel like making a really professional job of it, because you will no doubt need it for some time, especially if you are embarking on a new garden.

Fix the master-plan to a board and pin a piece of tracing paper over it. Then, all your drawing can be done on the tracing paper without defacing the master. You will probably want to do a lot of scribbling on the paper before you arrive at a scheme that fully satisfies you and you may want to scrap several pieces of tracing paper in the process.

If you are working on a new garden, the best bet is to

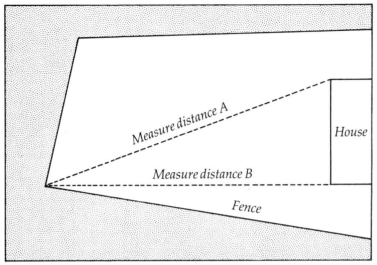

Fig. 1. To 'fix' any point on your plan, accurately measure from both corners of the house.

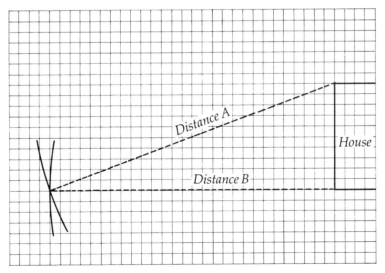

Fig 2. Now draw two arcs on squared paper to a predetermined scale. The point is fixed where they cross.

plan the whole scheme right from the start, even if you don't intend to do all the work immediately. Draw in your lawn, the patio, paths, walling and borders and any other features you intend to build. Fiddle around with the drawing until you are absolutely satisfied that the plan is exactly as you want it. It is much better to make mistakes at this stage than later.

Marking out

If you have drawn your plan on squared paper, transferring the plan to the site is a fairly simple matter. Start from one of your fixed points – again, the house is the easiest – measure up, and bang in a peg at, say, the corner of the patio. You may need to measure right-angles during the process of setting out, and this is where your 3,4,5 triangle will come in useful. Then, always working from the drawing, set out pegs at the remaining corners.

Now, join the pegs with string to show exactly the outline of the proposed feature. Then, take a walk around it looking from all angles. If it helps, go up and view it from the bedroom window, or from the sitting room if that is where you will see it when you're in the house. If it doesn't look right – change it. There is a golden rule in landscape design that 'if it *looks* right, it *is* right'. Because a plan looks good on paper, it doesn't necessarily follow that it will also look right when viewed from another angle, so that it doesn't offend the eye.

If your feature incorporates curves, the drawing and setting out process is a little more complicated. Start by drawing, either freehand, or with compasses or a drawing instrument known as a 'French curve'. When it comes to transferring this curve to the land, you must make a series of measurements from a fixed line (perhaps the boundary fence or the house) at intervals. Mark out these measurements with a peg, join them with string, and you have your curve.

Circles, of course, are easy, but make sure when you do the drawing, that you are able to locate exactly the centre

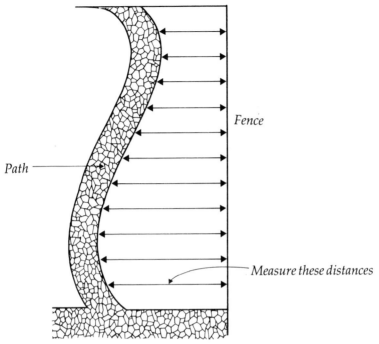

Fence

Path

Measure these distances

Fig 3. To mark out a curve on the ground, measure at fixed
intervals from a straight boundary.

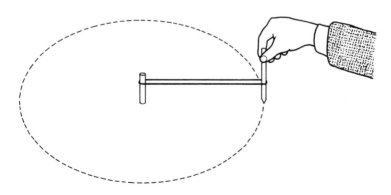

Fig 4. To mark out a circle, bang a peg into the centre and use a
loop of string.

of the circle. It's then an easy matter to bang in a peg, measure the radius of the circle from the plan, and mark it out with a piece of string and a sharpened stake.

With curves, even more than with straight lines, you may feel that you want to change the shape a little once you see it on the ground. Don't let that worry you at all. Remember, 'if it looks right, it *is* right'.

5 Preparation

If the site for your patio, path or walling is infested with weeds, it may well be worth while getting rid of them once and for all. Strong-growing perennial weeds can often push up paving and even crack concrete. If there is a vigorous tree nearby, such a as a poplar, sycamore or willow, then the roots will almost certainly cause you trouble.

If the weeds are only annuals, there is no point in wasting money on weedkillers. You will, in most cases, have a certain amount of excavation to do before you start on the stonework, and this will rid the site.

Invasive perennial weeds, such as couch grass, convolvulus, nettles, etc., should certainly be killed before any soil is excavated. Apart from the damage that any remaining roots would cause, there is no point in transferring the weeds from one part of the garden to another. This is only laying up trouble for the future.

I am a great believer in using a weedkiller that will not taint the soil and prevent anything growing for a long period. Certainly, it would be possible to use something cheap like sodium chlorate, but this does have its disadvantages. Firstly, it will make the soil unsuitable for growing for at least six months and possibly longer. This means that it cannot be carted to another part of the garden and used to make up a border or to level a new lawn area. It has the further disadvantage that it will 'creep' in the soil. If, for example, you are treating an area close to a border, even if you are careful not to allow the weedkiller to touch the cultivated soil, it will spread and damage plants.

If you wish to grow plants in the paved area, the roots

may well, at a later stage, reach down into the infected soil, and this will kill them. It is always worth spending a little more to avoid these hazards.

For perennial weeds, the material to use is called *glyphosate*. It is sold at present by Murphy Chemicals under the brand name 'Tumbleweed'. It can be applied with a watering can, but it is much better sprayed on with an ordinary garden sprayer. Not only does this save quite a bit of money because it puts less of the weedkiller on, but strangely enough, it is also more effective. The weedkiller is taken in by the leaves and translocated to the roots. Here it prevents them from storing or manufacturing food, so the plant dies. Naturally, it takes quite a time to show the effects, and you must leave at least a week for the weeds to absorb the herbicide, before starting to excavate. But then, you'll have a really clean site, and no worries for the future.

Trees are more of a problem. If they are vigorous and surface rooting like those already mentioned, the only answer is to pull them out. Bear in mind that they may also damage the foundations of the house if they are too close, in which case no time should be lost in removing them. If you do, make sure you plant at least one more tree in another part of your garden. Deeper rooting or less vigorous trees will cause no problems, and should be left in.

Excavating and levelling for paving

If you are laying even a small area of paving, it is important to find the correct levels and to allow for sufficient fall to take water away. After all, the paved area is often used specifically because grass can become too wet, so you won't want puddles.

If you are laying your patio next to the house, then correct levelling is of paramount importance. All modern houses, and many old ones too, have a damp-proof course (DPC) set in the brickwork just above ground level. This is there to prevent water from entering the bricks and rising up by capillary action. Without it, the water would even-

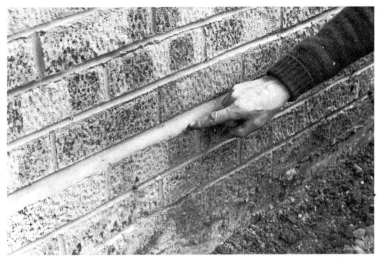

1. The damp-proof course can be easily recognized by the thicker layer of mortar between the bricks.

tually seep into the wall and reappear inside the house, with disastrous results.

It is quite easy to recognize the course of bricks in which the DPC has been embedded. The joint of mortar will be about twice the thickness of the other joints. On older houses, it was often the practice to use a layer of slates, or even a course of hard, blue engineering bricks, and of course, these can easily be seen.

Make sure that the finished level of the paving is at least two courses of bricks below the DPC. This will ensure that, even in heavy rain, no water splashes up above it.

If, as is sometimes the case with new houses, the builders have already laid a strip of concrete that finishes just two courses below the DPC, then I'm afraid there is no alternative but to dig it up again. Don't skimp by laying the paving on top of the concrete, or you may find yourself replastering the sitting room wall!

The first job is to mark out your patio area accurately allowing about 7.5cm(3in) extra all round. This will allow a small margin of error. Then, dig out the soil to a very rough level, carting the soil off the site.

Now you'll need a number of wooden pegs. These can be made out of rough, scrap wood, but should be fairly stout. Make them about 30–45cm(12–18in) long, and if you expect to take some time over the job it is worth giving them a coat of white paint. They will be there for the duration of the job and believe me, they are the easiest things in the world to trip over, so it's worth making them clearly visible.

Before banging in the pegs, mark a line on them to indicate the finished level of the concrete base. The position of the mark is easily worked out. Starting from the top of the peg, allow the thickness of the paving, plus an extra 2.5cm(1in) for the mortar bed. Thus, if the paving is 3.75cm(1½in) thick, the line should be marked 5.2cm(2½in) from the top of the peg. For 5cm(2in) thick paving, mark the line 7.5cm(3in) from the top.

Start by banging in the first peg near to the wall. Using the spirit level, make sure that it is at least two courses below the DPC. Now, using the straightedge and spirit level, bang in a line of pegs along the wall at exactly the same level.

2. Mark a line on the wooden pegs to allow for the thickness of the paving plus the depth of the mortar.

3. Start by banging the first peg in close to the wall, and make sure it is well below the damp-proof course.

4. Now the second row of pegs can be set, ensuring that there is a gentle fall away from the house.

The second row of pegs is set a distance away from the wall in line with the first row to form a right-angle with the house wall. Bear in mind when setting this row, that a slight fall will be needed.

The fall need not be great, and generally about 2.5cm(1in) in 3m(10ft) is sufficient. If your second row of pegs is 1.5m(5ft) from the first row, then they should be set about 13mm(½in) lower. To do this, simply cut a small scrap of wood 13mm(½in) thick, and place it on the top of the peg to be set. Then with your straightedge running from the peg nearest the house to the one you are levelling, tap down the peg until the spirit level shows it exactly level. Remove the piece of 13mm(½in) wood, and the peg will be at the correct level. The remainder of the row can be set from this peg. It is a good idea to check the odd peg here and there with those in the first row, using your scrap of wood. At this stage, you can't be too careful.

When all the pegs are in, make sure that you warn the other members of your family that they are there. Tripping over one peg and landing on another can cause a nasty injury and worse, it may upset your levels!

Having set all the pegs, you can now accurately dig out to the correct levels for concrete. If you are making a patio that will only be used for pedestrian traffic, and the soil is well consolidated, you will need a concrete base no more than 7.5cm(3in) thick. If the soil has been deeply cultivated, or contains a high proportion of organic matter, 10cm(4in) is better. Bear in mind, also, that builder's excavations will always settle, however well they are beaten down afterwards. This is especially so round new houses where the footings have been dug out by machine and refilled later.

In this case it may be better to dig out deeply and refill with about 30cm(1ft) of well-consolidated hardcore covered by 15cm(6in) of concrete. This is also necessary if you are building a driveway that will have to take vehicles.

Work out the necessary depth of concrete or hardcore and concrete and dig out to leave that thickness below the line marked on the pegs. When digging out, try not to dig too deeply so that you have to refill later. If you do make a mistake, refill with hardcore and tamp it down well. If you refill with soil, it will always settle a little, leaving spaces beneath the concrete base.

The soil you dig out can generally be used somewhere else in the garden, but there may be times when it is better to cart it away. Many builders dig out the footings for the

5. When digging out around the pegs, try not to dig too deeply so that the soil has to be refilled.

house and simply leave the subsoil on top of the existing topsoil. This is always best carted away, since it is worse than useless spread on top of the garden soil.

Because you may wish to use the soil on another part of the garden, it can be seen that if you are embarking on a new garden it is best to do all the 'hard' landscaping first.

Levelling for walls

The preparation for walling is much the same, except that the depth of concrete for the footing will vary according to the height of the wall. For a wall under 1m(3ft) high, the concrete need only be about 10cm(4in) thick, but for higher walls, you should allow at least 15cm(6in).

The width of the footing is also important. It must be at least twice the width of the proposed wall. So, if you are building a single brick wall, make the footing at least 23cm(9in) wide. For a double brick wall, it should be 45cm(18in) wide. The top of the pegs in this case, are used to show the finished level of the concrete footing, and they should finish a couple of inches below soil level, so that no concrete shows.

Bear in mind also that walling is always built level. The footing should never slope. If the ground slopes, it will be necessary to 'step' the footings, and the steps should be in multiples of the thickness of your brick or stone.

6. Footings for walls must be dug out deeper and should be at least twice the width of the wall.

6 Drainage

A large expanse of paving will trap a great deal of water. Very often, the patio at the back of the house will be as big as one side of the house roof, and will collect as much rainwater. It is important to allow for this to get away.

Firstly, though it has been said before in previous chapters, it *must* be remembered that the paving should slope away from the house. The slope need not be great enough to be noticeable, but it should be sufficient to ensure that, even in a flash storm, the water has no chance to build up against the wall of the house.

Very often, provided this is borne in mind, drainage is no problem. If, for example, the paving slopes away to a flower border, the water will simply run off the surface and into the flower bed. In wet areas, you may have to bear this

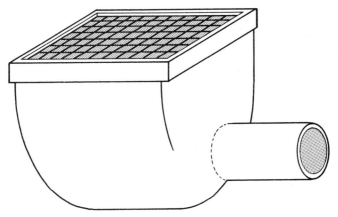

Fig 1. A gulley trap which can be bought at the builder's merchants. Set it in the patio.

in mind when planting the border, since it will generally be wetter than other parts of the garden.

If the patio slopes down to grass, there is a chance that water may be trapped. When building the patio, it should be made at such a level that the grass is very slightly proud of the paving. This will enable the mower to cut right to the edge without difficulty, and the edges will be no problem to cut. The grass will, however, form a natural barrier to escaping water.

If this is the case, dig out a trench about 15cm(6in) deep and 30cm(1ft) wide at the edge of the paving before levelling the soil for the lawn.

The trench should be filled with a suitable drainage material, such as crushed clinker or gravel, before covering with about 7.5cm(3in) of soil. This sort of depth will be quite enough for the grass, and will provide an adequate drain for excess water. If the soil is very heavy and natural drainage poor, the width and depth of the drain can be increased.

So far, so good. But the problems really start to arise when the garden slopes up away from the house. In this case, it may be necessary to build a retaining wall at the far end of the patio. It can be clearly seen that this creates a

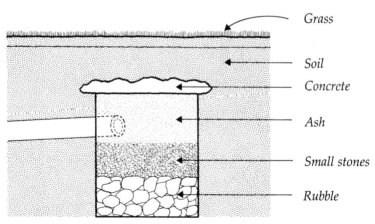

Grass

Soil

Concrcte

Ash

Small stones

Rubble

Fig 2. Dig a large soakaway in the garden to take all the excess water from the patio.

well that, if no provision were made, would turn into an impromptu swimming pool at every shower of rain. In this case it is necessary to make special provision to take the water away. Thought must be given to this at a very early stage in the building of the patio, since drainage must be one of the first jobs.

On most patios, only one drain will be necessary, but if the area of paving is very large, it may warrant two. Start by selecting a point somewhere near the middle of the patio at the end furthest from the house, for the gulley that will collect the excess water. When setting your level pegs, you must ensure that they slope not only away from the house, but also from either end towards the centre, where the gulley will be set.

The water is collected by means of a glazed earthenware gulley trap. They are easily obtainable at any good builder's merchant. From the outlet of the gulley trap, set a number of earthenware drainage pipes to a soakaway in the garden.

The soakaway can be either under the lawn or in a flower border. Bear in mind that, if it is sited in the border, you will probably need to sink it lower to allow for a sufficient depth of soil to accommodate plants. Under the lawn, a covering of about 15cm(6in) of soil will be enough.

The soakaway is built by digging a large pit. Naturally, the larger the patio, the larger the pit should be. The hole is filled with rubble at the bottom, covered by a depth of gravel with a covering of concrete over the top to prevent soil filtering down and blocking the drain.

If you are building a retaining wall, bear in mind also that the water will be pushing against the back of the wall too. Unless provision is made for it to escape, the water could build up to such an extent in a wet season, that the pressure could push the wall over. To avoid this, build in 'weep holes' in the brick or stonework, to allow the water to escape. The simplest way to do this is to leave a space in the second row of bricks at about 1m(1yd) intervals. However, the finished effect will be much more attractive if earthenware drainage pipes are set in the spaces.

Avoid the temptation to plant these all-important 'safety-valves' since roots of plants can mass together to choke the hole and block the escaping water.

However, on high walls that are built to retain soil on the other side, it is a good idea to leave a few more holes at intervals higher up the wall, specifically for plants. Though the roots will prevent some water escaping, their combined effect will certainly contribute something to the drainage, and they will look attractive into the bargain.

One final point on drainage that should be borne in mind at the planning stage. If you intend to lay an area of uneven surface, like cobbles or stable blocks, remember that it is much more difficult to provide adequate drainage. They should therefore not be laid in areas where it is important to maintain a dry surface.

7 Concreting

A knowledge of concrete and concreting is essential for all 'hard' landscaping work. If you are laying the base for a paved patio the finish need only be rough, but the principles are much the same. If you are concreting a driveway or a path the finish must be good and the work thorough if a really strong result is to be obtained.

Shuttering

A base for paving requires no shuttering to keep the concrete within bounds and to form a neat, finished edge. But for a driveway, where the edge of the concrete will be seen, it is essential.

Generally, for domestic jobs, the shuttering can be made out of wood. It is possible to hire metal 'formers' but these can be expensive and the depth of concrete required is not usually enough to warrant them. Normally, 10cm × 2.5cm(4in × 1in) sawn timber will be adequate for paths. For driveways, where a greater depth of concrete is required, use 15cm × 2.5cm (6in × 1in).

The shuttering is nailed to pegs driven into the ground at about 1m(3ft) intervals. Make sure that the shuttering is nailed to the *inside* of the pegs, so that they are not concreted in. This way, the finish of the edge is neater, and the shuttering can be removed afterwards. If the path or driveway is to be curved, the timber can easily be bent by making a series of saw-cuts on the inside of the curve.

When you are setting the shuttering, make sure that it is level from side to side, and that the slope (if there is one) is even.

For a driveway that is to take vehicles, you will need to set a layer of hardcore underneath the concrete, so dig out for this inside the shuttering after you have set it. Generally, 15cm(6in) of hardcore, well compacted, will be sufficient. Hardcore can consist of builders rubble, generally obtainable from demolition sites, or of crushed stone from the quarry.

Concrete

Once the shuttering is in position, and the hardcore down, the concrete can be ordered. Before doing so, make sure that you have the necessary tools for the job to hand. For a driveway, it is advisable to use a vibrating board. This consists of a long board with a handle on each end. Set on top of the board is an engine that serves to vibrate it as you move it along. This useful piece of equipment can be hired from most small tool hirers, and will make the job easier, stronger and very well finished. You will also need a shovel and the help of a friend or neighbour.

1. The easiest way to buy concrete is readi-mix, but you will have to be well organized.

The easiest way to buy concrete is ready-mixed. This saves a lot of back-breaking work, but it has two disadvantages. Firstly it is more expensive than mixing your own, but perhaps more importantly, you need to be well organized before it arrives. Don't, for example, do as a friend of mine did. He realized only when he had a 10-tonne load of wet concrete in the middle of his driveway that he had left his car in the garage! He was without the use of it for several days.

Make sure that everything is ready, and you'll save yourself a lot of work. One other advantage with ready-mix, is that the merchant will know exactly what sort of mix you require for your particular job, so you'll cut out one of the biggest causes of mistakes.

If you decide to mix your own, it is well worth hiring a small mixer if you have any amount to do. Not only is the work reduced to an acceptable minimum, but it will make a better job of the mixing too. For small areas, of course, the mixing can be done by hand.

Concrete for paths, driveways and the base for a patio is made up with sharp sand, aggregate (gravel) and cement. It is easiest to buy the sand and aggregate already mixed, and most merchants will be able to supply it. To decide how much you need, start by measuring the area to be covered. This is then multiplied by the depth of concrete required to give the volume required. Most builder's merchants will be able to translate this into tonnes of aggregate (discount the volume of cement, which makes little or no difference). As an example, 1 tonne(1ton) of aggregate will give 12sq.m(12sq.yds) of concrete 7.5cm(3in) thick. If the concrete is to be 15cm(6in) thick, it will naturally cover half this area. For each tonne of aggregate, you will need eight bags of cement.

For a driveway or for the base of paving or walling, the concrete should be made by mixing eight parts by volume of aggregate with one part of Portland cement.

When mixing concrete, remember that the drier the mix is, the stronger will be the concrete when it sets. So, you should make the mix as dry as possible, consistent with it being workable. For a smooth finish, it will have to be much wetter than that used for the base for paving. Where this sort of rough finish is all that is necessary, the concrete can in fact be put down dry. Moisture from the soil beneath will eventually ensure that the concrete sets hard.

2. If you have a large amount to mix, it is well worthwhile hiring a small concrete mixer.

3. To hand-mix concrete, start by adding the cement to the aggregate and turning it thoroughly.

4. Make a hole in the middle of the heap and add water. Remember to make it as dry as you can work with.

5. Now push some of the outside of the heap of aggregate into the middle of the hole.

6. Finish mixing by thoroughly turning the heap again, making sure all the mixture is evenly wet.

7. To make a path, start by setting the shuttering, levelling across with a straightedge and spirit level.

8. Fill inside the shuttering with concrete and tamp down with a piece of timber. Finish with a 'sawing' action.

9. At the end of the day, cover what you have done with sacking and block the end with wood, giving a clean start the next day.

10. If you wish to make a textured finish, simply mark lines in the hardening cement with a broom.

11. For a smooth finish, the surface should be stroked gently with a metal plasterer's float.

12. Concrete for a paving base need not be well finished. Barrow it onto the site, avoiding the pegs.

13. Spread the concrete around, making sure that it comes no higher than the mark on the pegs.

54

14. For this sort of base, it is sufficient so consolidate the concrete by treading it down.

For a driveway or a path that is not to be paved afterwards, the mix should be wetter. The concrete is then poured into the shuttered area, and the board worked backwards and forwards across the top of the shuttering until the 'fat' rises to the top to form a good surface. This way, the finished surface of the concrete will be slightly ribbed, and it is worth leaving it like this to make a non-slip surface. If you require a smooth surface, you will have to go over it with a plasterer's float afterwards.

Once the concrete is down, it must be 'cured'. This is done by covering the surface with wet sacking or hessian, to ensure that it dries slowly. It will be much stronger this way. Curing is unnecessary when laying the base for paving. All you need do is to rake out the dry concrete so that it comes up to the line previously marked on the pegs, and consolidate it by treading. Make sure that the base never comes over the marked line, or you may not be able to knock the paving slabs down low enough to level them.

When concreting for the foundations of walling, the

trench itself should retain the concrete, so there is no need for shuttering. Bring the concrete up to the top of the pegs, and tamp it down well with a baulk of timber. Though a really fine finish is unnecessary, the top should be reasonably smooth and level.

If you are concreting in the winter when there is a danger of frost, make sure that you can cover the whole area at night, or mix a proprietary concrete anti-freeze in with the mixing water.

8 Rectangular paving

There is no doubt that for the do-it-yourselfer, artificial rectangular paving slabs are the favourite method of making a path or patio. They are reasonably inexpensive, they look good, and they are certainly the easiest to lay.

The first job is to decide on the pattern of laying them. It is a fairly simple matter to work out a pattern on paper first, in which case, as has already been suggested, it will be easier to order just the quantity you require. Alternatively, they can be laid in an entirely random fashion, working out the pattern as you go along. To work this way you will have to think three or four slabs ahead in order to avoid long 'tramlines', but once you get the hang of it, it is not difficult.

The mortar

Slabs are laid on a mortar made with three parts of soft builders sand to one of Portland cement. When mixing, it is important not to make the mix too wet. If it is, the mortar will 'slump' when the slabs are rested on it, and they will be difficult, if not impossible, to level. Again, if the weather is likely to be frosty, mix a little anti-freeze in with the water.

Before starting, get yourself a 'spot-board'. This is simply a piece of timber large enough to take a fair pile of mortar. It will save you a lot of waste mortar. Never try to scoop the mortar out of a bucket. That way it's difficult and very frustrating. It's also a good idea to put a few slabs of different sizes to hand. This will save a lot of walking about once you get started.

Laying the slabs

The first slab is definitely the most important, since this sets the pattern of level and line for all the rest. It is well worth taking a lot of trouble over this one. Get it right and you'll have no problems with the rest.

Start by placing five mounds of mortar on the base where the slab is to lay. They should be at each corner with one, slightly smaller mound in the centre.

Lift the slab and place it on the mounds. Never try to lower it on while one side of the slab is resting on the ground. This way you will flatten two of the mounds of mortar, and levelling will be difficult.

When the slab is resting on the mortar, check that it is aligned correctly. This is most important, especially if the slabs are adjacent to the house wall. If the first slab of a long patio or path is just the slightest bit out of line, by the time you reach the other end it will be several inches out. To allow for a small margin of error, set the first slab about 2.5cm(1in) away from the wall.

Then set up a line so that it runs along the top edge of the slab, nearest to the wall. Take the line to the other end and fix it so that it, too, is 2.5cm(1in) from the wall. Now it is an easy matter to ensure that the top of the slab is exactly in line with the line.

Now the slab must be levelled. Place the straightedge on top at one end, and on the nearest peg at the other. Tap it down with the handle of the club hammer until the straightedge lies exactly flat along the top of the slab. Always use the *handle* of a hammer for tapping down the slabs since the metal head is very likely to crack it. You will probably find, at the end of the job, that you need a new handle, but that is a small price to pay if all the slabs are intact.

If the slab is meant to be level one way, it is worth checking it with the spirit level at this stage. It will, of course, slope away from the house, so the level will not register true that way.

The second and subsequent slabs are laid in exactly the

1. Mix the mortar and set out five small heaps where the first slab is to be laid.

2. The slab is now rested on top of the heaps of mortar a little way away from the wall.

3. Tap the slab down carefully until it is exactly level with the nearest peg.

4. Now, using the straightedge, make sure it is also level the other way.

5. It is important to ensure that the first slab is exactly in line with the wall.

6. With the first slab correctly positioned, the remaining slabs can now be laid.

same way, butting them up tight with the last slab laid. Generally, if you are using artificial slabs, there is no need to leave a space for pointing. Indeed, the crack between the slabs will serve to take any surface water away quickly. If you are laying natural stone paving, you may find that the edges are not even enough to allow close butting. In this case, leave a gap of about 13mm(½in) and point it in with mortar afterwards.

If you are working to a pattern, keep the plan handy, and it is a simple matter to select the next slab you need by referring to the plan. If you are working out the pattern as you go along, you will need to think ahead. It is important to avoid long, straight lines, so as soon as you see a line becoming unacceptably long, 'break' it by placing the next slab across it.

As the paving proceeds, check regularly with the straightedge that the slabs are level with the pegs. There is no need, of course, to check for alignment after the first slab is laid, since this decides the line for all the others.

As you come to a peg and it is in the way, either break it off, or drive it down into the concrete base.

When you have set each slab, try to 'rock' it on its heaps of mortar. Inevitably, some slabs will rock, and the only thing to do then is to take them up and lay them again.

Cutting slabs

Inevitably, there will be obstructions in the paving, like a gulley surround or an inspection cover, and this may well mean that slabs will have to be cut. If you are using straight concrete slabs, you will, I'm afraid, find them very difficult to cut with a hammer and chisel. In this case, it is best to hire a special stone saw. These consist of a motorized cutting disc, and they will cut through concrete quite easily.

Slabs made with stone chipping aggregate can be cut with a hammer and a brick bolster. Cutting them in half is surprisingly easy, but if you have to cut out an intricate shape, be prepared to break a few at first.

7. As the pegs get in the way of the next slab, tap them down or knock them out.

8. It is a good practice to keep the broom in use continually to prevent mortar stains.

9. At the end of the days work, clean up the mortar at the edge of each slab.

10. The final job is to point in between the slabs and the wall with dryish mortar.

Start by measuring up the slab and marking the line of the cut on the face (upper) side. Tip the slab on its side and cut a nick in each edge. Using the nick as a guide, mark the line of the cut on the reverse side of the slab.

Now lean the slab up against your leg and cut down the mark carefully with the hammer and brick bolster. Tap fairly gently, to cut a slight nick in the slab. Turn the slab round, and repeat the operation on the reverse side. Then turn it round again and cut the front line again, repeating the process until the slab falls in half. It really is not as difficult as it sounds. The secret lies in knowing just how hard to tap, and in having the patience to do the job gradually and slowly. Unless you are a very handy handyman (or woman), you can be sure that you will break the odd slab or two before you finally get the knack of cutting, so make sure you allow for a few breakages in your initial order.

If you find that cutting is impossible, or if you are working with concrete slabs, the alternative is to fill the awkward spaces with cement when the paving is completed. You can buy cement colouring powders, so that the concrete can be matched in colour to the slabs, making a fairly unobtrusive job.

As you progress with the paving, keep a soft broom handy. This is one of the more important tools in your kit and its use should not be neglected. If you drop a bit of mortar on the surface of the slabs, wait until it dries, but sweep it off before it hardens.

If you cannot finish the whole job in one day, make sure that, before you pack up for the night, you cut away any excess mortar that might be squeezing out from underneath the slabs. If you allow it to harden, you will have to chisel it away before you can lay the next slab

Pointing

If you have laid the paving with spaces between the slabs, they will have to be pointed in. This is done with a slightly stronger mortar, mixing two parts of sand to one of cement. The mortar can be worked in between the slabs

11. To cut paving, mark a line on the face of the slab and then cut a groove in each edge.

12. Leaning the slab against your leg, gently tap with the club hammer and brick bolster, both sides of the slab.

with a trowel and smoothed over. This is quite a time-consuming job, however. A quicker way is to brush the dry mix into the spaces. Make sure that the slabs are perfectly dry when you do this or the mortar will stain them. When all the spaces are filled, cover the entire area with about 13mm(½in) of soft sand, and lightly water it. Later the sand can be brushed off again, and the job's done.

Once the paving is down, it is vital that it should not be trodden on for several days. Make sure that you warn your family and friends and, to make doubly sure, put a few obstructions in the way to remind them. The wheelbarrow with the straightedge leaning against it is generally sufficient.

Finally, when you have finished each evening, and even before you take time to stand back and admire your handiwork, make sure that you wash all your tools thoroughly. Believe me, nothing is worse than trying to work with tools that are caked in cement, or humping a barrow with half a hundredweight of hard cement stuck to it. Don't forget, particularly, to wash the barrow wheel. This is often forgotten and only makes for a hard life.

9 Paving on sand

Who hasn't seen local authority paviors laying pavement slabs on sand? Certainly this is common practice and pavements rarely have to be replaced. This has led to the common belief that laying slabs on sand is perfectly adequate in all circumstances. Not true. In fact, it is fraught with dangers.

Firstly, the men you have watched laying slabs in the streets are experts. It really is not at all easy to level slabs that are set in sand. This necessitates getting just the right thickness of sand underneath the slab so that, when it is tapped down, it is exactly level with its neighbours and will not sink further. That sort of judgement takes a lot of experience.

But the main disadvantage with laying on sand is that the ground beneath it invariably sinks. Pavements are often laid either on soil that has been compacted by millions of pairs of feet over the years, or on a deep layer of hardcore that has been rolled with a really heavy road roller to compact it solid. Not easy in your back garden. This is particularly so when paving is being laid next to a new house. Invariably, the footings for the building are taken out with a mechanical digger. This digs a trench much too wide, and is refilled afterwards. However much the soil is then compacted, it will *always* sink a little, and the paving will end up at all different levels. This makes it dangerous and unsightly. So, unless the soil underneath the paving has been well compacted over a period of years, or you can provide a deep, well-consolidated layer of hardcore, play safe and lay the slabs on concrete as described in the previous chapter.

Provided all these conditions are fulfilled, then laying on sand is feasible. Use sharp sand, and mix a little dry Portland cement in with it at the ratio of about six to one. This will 'stabilize' the sand and help prevent it sinking.

Set the first slab as described previously but, instead of placing it on five points of mortar, make the sand bed level underneath the whole slab. The depth of the bed should be such that the slab has to be tapped down well to get it level. Because more tapping down is needed, it is unwise to use slabs less than 5cm(2in) thick, as many breakages are bound to occur. Ideally, go for 5cm(2in) slabs that have been made on a press as opposed to in a mould.

Align the slab to the wall, and check for level against the nearest peg, exactly as described for laying on mortar. With the first slab down, it will be a little easier to judge the amount of sand needed for the next one to allow for full compaction. But it must be stressed that this is the most difficult part of the job, and you must be prepared to take up a few and re-lay them if they are not level or compacted enough.

Slabs laid on sand *must* be pointed in between. This means that a space must be left between each slab to allow for the concrete fillet. To make sure that the space is exactly the same each time, it's a good idea to cut some pieces of wood about 13mm(½in) thick to place between each slab to guage the space accurately. The pointing in is important to add strength, and to prevent water washing through between the slabs and washing the sand out. For the same reason, it is necessary to cement a fillet right round the edge of the paving to prevent the sand washing out from underneath.

The mortar for the pointing is made with two parts by volume of soft builders sand, to one part Portland cement. It can be put in wet with a trowel, or brushed in dry, though naturally, that used for the fillet round the edge must be trowelled in.

When mixing the mortar for pointing, unless the whole lot can be done in one go, it is wise to mix it accurately by measuring it out with a bucket. If it is simply roughly measured by the shovel-full, the quantities will vary with each mix, and the colour of the resulting pointing will also vary.

Finally, remember when laying slabs on sand, that the paving will be suitable for pedestrian traffic only. Never, never run the car over them, or they will almost certainly move and will probably crack.

10 Stepping stones

Sometimes, it is necessary to make a path in the lawn. It may be to run alongside the washing-line, or it may be for access across the garden. It may even be desirable to do so for purely aesthetic reasons. Well done, paths can look attractive.

If your land is on the heavy side, it is quite likely that the soil will lay wet. Constant traffic, especially in the winter, will soon make bare patches in the grass, and these will quickly be colonized by weeds and moss. In this case, some sort of hard path is essential.

1. Lay out the stepping stones first and walk across them to ensure they are in the right place.

2. Cut round the slab with a spade or edging tool, and lift out the turf.

But it is often a mistake, especially in a small garden, to cut the lawn up into strips with a solid path. This has the visual effect of making the garden appear smaller and is rarely easy on the eye. One way round this problem is to lay stepping stones with grass strips in between to give the feeling of continuity across the lawn.

Stepping-stone paths can be straight or curved, depending on the design of the garden. But above all, they should be comfortable to walk on. There is nothing more annoying than to walk down a stepping-stone path that is so designed that, even if you start out with your feet on the first slab, you finish up walking on the grass in between.

To get over this, start by laying the slabs on the grass and actually walking on them. This exercise will also give you the opportunity to look carefully at the path, and to move the slabs about until the most pleasing effect is obtained.

With the slabs laid in position, it is an easy matter to cut round them with a sharp spade or a half-moon edging tool.

3. Place a little sand in the bottom of the hole to enable you to level the slab easily.

Then lift the slab, and remove the turf underneath it. Try to take the turf with just enough soil to enable you to lay about 2.5cm(1in) of sand and leave the stone a little below the grass level. Bear in mind that the lawn will have to be cut, and that the mower will need to ride over the top of the slabs. Otherwise, you will be letting yourself in for a lot of extra work.

Mix the sand with a little cement, and tap the slab down onto the bed so that it is level. Eventually, the edges of the grass will break down a little, and you may need to trim them back from time to time with the edging tool.

4. Tap the slab down so that the surface is just a little below the level of the grass.

11 Crazy paving

Think carefully before you decide to lay crazy paving. It is certainly cheaper than rectangular paving, especially if you buy it from the local council yard. But it will only give a pleasing effect in certain situations. Generally it can be said that it just doesn't fit in with modern architecture. Somehow it looks too fussy and old fashioned. In the garden of an older house, however, it can look quite attractive, especially if little pockets are left for plants. All sorts of alpine and rock plants can be grown in a crazy-paving path to make a strip of living colour.

If you can run to it, buy natural stone paving. Split York-stone is very attractive and because it can be obtained in quite thin pieces it is only a fraction of the price of natural rectangular paving. However, what you save on the cost of the paving you will lose again to some extent on the extra sand and cement necessary. Crazy paving must, in the main, be laid on a solid bed of mortar, so you will certainly need more sand.

Lay the base in exactly the same way as recommended for rectangular paving, using concrete if there is any chance of sinkage. Don't forget to put in the pegs for levelling. The mortar is made as for rectangular paving using a 3/1 mix of soft sand and cement.

Start by selecting a few larger pieces. These are laid first round the edges of the area to be laid. The largest pieces can be laid on five points of mortar but smaller lumps must be set on a solid bed. Remember that if you are using split, natural paving that has been cut quite thin, it will not take a lot of weight. So this, too, is best laid on a solid bed.

When laying the slabs, leave a space in between each

piece to allow for pointing in. Because the pieces are not of a uniform shape, the spaces will be irregular, but they should be made to fit as nearly as possible.

1. Lay large pieces with straight edges on the outside and fill in with smaller pieces, tapping them down level.

Once the outside pieces are laid, fill in the middle, selecting pieces at random. Now this is the bit that really does drive you crazy. Fitting the pieces together is rather like doing a jigsaw puzzle and it can be just as time-consuming. Don't even attempt to sort through the stack each time you need a bit to fit a certain place. Keep a club hammer and a chisel nearby, select a piece that nearly fits, and chop off the odd corner that is out of shape. Otherwise, you'll probably shift that stack of paving dozens of times before you're finished.

As before, keep the straightedge in use all the time to check levels. This is not as easy with natural paving as with artificial, because the stones do not have a smooth, regular surface. In this case, you will have to be content with a slightly less level surface. A little water will be bound to lodge on the top of natural crazy paving. I think it looks attractive, but if it worries you, you will have to make the overall slope a little sharper.

2. Check regularly that the individual pieces are level, and run the straightedge from the stones to the pegs.

Once the paving has set hard – generally after about two days – it should be pointed in. Don't attempt to do this job too early, or you will find that the pieces move as you tread on them and this will naturally upset the levels.

Pointing in can be done with soft sand, or if you want a stronger joint use sharp sand. Soft sand is perhaps better if you are using a natural stone, such as York, because it will better match the colour of the stone. Sharp sand looks greyer when set, and is therefore best to use with concrete or granite slabs.

3. The finished path should be pointed in with mortar and then 'lined out' for a really neat finish.

Mix the mortar as before, using a 2/1 mix of sand and cement and a bucket to measure the materials accurately. With crazy paving, the pointing cannot be done by brushing in a dry mix. Make the mortar fairly sloppy so that it will work well with a trowel. Place it on a spot-board near where you are working, and put it in with a small pointing trowel.

The mortar should be worked well down between he slabs with the edge of the trowel, and then smoothed to give a nice, clean surface level with the top of the stones.

The finish of the pointing is important, since this will set off the paving. There are two popular ways of finishing it off. Either the trowel is run down the line of cement at an angle so that it is raised slightly towards the middle, or it is marked out with lines. Lining out is done after the mortar has dried, but before it is set solid. Don't leave it too long, or you may find that it has set too hard.

Lining is best done with a stout piece of wire bent into a U shape. An ideal tool for the job is a bricklayer's butterfly. This is a piece of wire, shaped like a pair of butterfly wings, that is used to tie two walls together. Bricklayers use (and lose) hundreds of them in the course of building a house, so if your house is new you may well find several knocking about the site. If not, your friendly builder's merchant will no doubt be pleased to give you one.

When you do the lining out, you will probably find that it throws up small 'crumbs' of mortar that look rather unsightly. Don't worry about these. They will brush off with a soft brush the following day. If you have slopped a bit of mortar onto the stones, it will stain and look ugly. It can be removed by brushing the surface of the stones with a wire brush once the mortar is hard.

If there is any danger of frost, either put a drop of concrete anti-freeze into the mixing water, or cover the whole area with hessian or paper.

12 Bricks

Bricks make a very attractive path in most gardens, or they can be used infilled into rectangular paving to create an interesting texture pattern. They are also a very versatile medium, since they can be used in a variety of patterns to form squares or circles, straight lines to break the monotony of square paving, or in curves.

It is, however, essential to use the right kind of bricks. Never use ordinary fletton bricks or sand-faced flettons, such as those used to build walls. These are made specially to be used vertically, where water will run off them immediately. If they are used on the flat, water lies on them and

1. Bricks make an attractive and durable paving material, but you must be sure to choose the right types.

penetrates the brick. At the first frost the water will expand and the surface of the brick will flake. The only bricks that are suitable for paving are stock bricks or the very hard engineering bricks. Bought new, both types will cost a lot of money, but it is generally possible to pick up second-hand stock or engineering bricks from the demolition contractor much more cheaply. They will also be weathered and will look much more mellow and attractive.

To lay them, make the base in the same way as described for rectangular paving, not forgetting the level pegs. Like crazy paving, they should be set on a solid bed of mortar. Being small, they are slightly more difficult to level, though a certain amount of gentle undulation is often acceptable provided there is enough slope to take away excess water.

If the bricks are being used as an infill in paving, levelling is no problem. Set the paving first, leaving out a space where the bricks are to go. By simply placing the straight-edge from slab to slab, the bricks can easily be tapped down to the correct level. For larger areas, level pegs are used exactly as for rectangular paving.

Leave a space of about 13mm(½in) between bricks to allow for pointing. Inevitably, you will find that bricks have to be cut, but this is an easy matter with a brick bolster and club hammer.

When the paving is completed, it must be pointed. The best way to do this is to brush in a dry mix of sand and cement mixed in a ratio of 2/1. Again, make sure that the bricks are perfectly dry before doing this, and cover the whole area with about 2.5cm(1in) of soft sand before watering over the top in a fine spray. Afterwards, the sand is brushed off to leave a clean finish.

If you decide to lay bricks in a circle it is important to line them up properly so that the edge of each brick faces into the centre of the circle. Start by deciding on the size and position of the circle, and bang a stout peg into the centre. Tie a piece of string the length of the circle's radius to the peg, and mark out for the base. Set the concrete for the foundation, leaving the centre peg and the string in position. The edge of each brick can then be lined up, using the string. If your circle is round a tree (and this can look very attractive) the string must be looped rather than tied round the trunk so that it will move round it. Otherwise it will shorten as you move it round.

Cobbles

Cobbles are large round or oval stones, generally of granite. When set, they are naturally difficult and uncomfortable to walk on, so the siting of them must be planned carefully. Don't put cobbles in a place that will get a lot of use or where garden furniture is to be set up, since the surface will be very uneven. Indeed, they are often used specifically to discourage pedestrian traffic, in places where it is desirable to prevent people walking.

It is naturally impossible to level cobbles accurately, but since they are usually only used as infills in rectangular paving, this presents few problems.

Set them in sharp sand, again using the 3/1 ratio of sand and cement. They are set in rows, and tapped down individually with a club hammer. Make the mix fairly dry, or you will find that, as you tap down one stone, another already previously laid pops up.

Pointing of cobbles is impossible and unnecessary. All you need to do is to brush between them with a soft handbrush when the mortar is getting dry, but before it gets hard. This will be sufficient to give a level enough surface. The mortar should finish about 2.5cm(1in) below the level of the tops of the cobbles.

Setts and stable blocks

Granite setts are generally cubes of stone, and are used particularly in road building. It is possible to buy them new, but second-hand setts are normally freely available and very much cheaper. It is now possible to buy concrete setts that are a very good imitation of the real thing, but very much thinner, and therefore even cheaper.

82

2. Cobbles can be used as an infill in rectangular paving or to discourage pedestrian traffic.

They, like bricks, are a very versatile medium because of their small size. They can be used as infills in paving, in straight lines, squares, rectangles or circles. They are laid in exactly the same way as bricks.

Stable blocks are made of the same material as engineering bricks, giving a dark grey, almost black finish. These are generally laid in a square pattern and look very attractive set in paving or on their own. It is possible to buy them second-hand, though they are quite difficult to come by. Alternatively, the same effect can be had by using block paving. This gives the same effect as stable blocks but is laid in exactly the same way as rectangular paving. Again, they are more expensive than normal paving, and are generally used as an infill.

To avoid the garish effect of white pointing with these dark coloured blocks, it is best to colour the pointing mortar with a grey cement colourant.

Paving blocks

A new concept in paving has recently been introduced with the express aim of simplifying the job for the do-it-yourselfer. Frankly, I wonder whether it is, in fact, easier to do than straightforward rectangular paving. But the end result is certainly very attractive and the problem of levelling is reduced to a minimum.

The system uses rectangular concrete blocks that look very much like bricks, except in colour. The area to be paved is first edged with wooden shuttering, which is levelled with a spirit-level. Soft sand is then spread inside the shuttering and levelled off by drawing a board backwards and forwards across the shuttering in much the same way as described for concreting. The blocks are then set out in a pre-chosen pattern on the sand. Don't tamp them down at this stage.

When the whole area has been laid, you will have to hire a vibrating pad. These consist of a machine with a large plate on the bottom. When the engine is started, the pad

3. Concrete blocks are easy to lay and can, like bricks, be set in a variety of patterns.

84

4. After laying, they are pointed with a dry mix, and consolidated with a vibrating pad.

vibrates rapidly backwards and forwards, pressing down the blocks evenly as it goes. The vibrating action makes a very strong job of firming the blocks – even stronger if you 'stabilise' the sand using a mixture of six parts sand to one of cement. If sharp sand is used instead of soft, the finished paving should be strong enough to take a car.

After vibrating, brush in a mixture of two parts sand to one of cement and go over it again with the vibrating pad. This will work the pointing mix down quite a bit, so the operation may have to be repeated to top it up.

13 Inspection covers

What garden is not 'blessed' with at least one inspection cover? I have seen new, small gardens with as many as five! They are necessary, of course, to allow access to drains and sewage pipes, so it is essential that they should not be covered with paving. The answer is to incorporate them into the paving and, with a little ingenuity, this is not as difficult as it sounds.

The problem is, that they are very rarely set in line with your paving and you will be very lucky indeed to find them set at the correct level. They will generally have to be raised or lowered so that the top of the cover is exactly level with the surface of the paving.

Unless the cover is so low as to be below the level of the concrete base for the paving, the area can be pegged level and the concrete put in first. If it is below the concrete level it will have to be raised first. It is possible to do the whole job before the paving is laid, levelling the top of the cover to the pegs, but I prefer to wait until the paving reaches the manhole. This way you could save yourself quite a bit of cutting round the cover.

Start by removing the lid. Old covers were equipped with metal lifting rings, but new ones generally have two slots at the ends, to take a special key. If you don't have a key, it is relatively simple to lift the cover by inserting a trowel between the cover and the frame and levering it up.

The frame will be cemented to the brickwork and this should now be removed. Before starting work, make sure that no-one in your family is likely to flush the lavatory or empty the bath, and place an old sack in the hole to catch any bits of mortar, and prevent the drain becoming blocked.

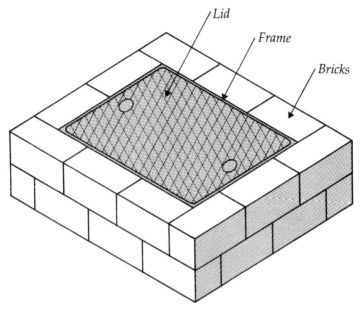

To lower an inspection cover, remove the lid, chip out the frame and remove a course of bricks. Then refit the frame and replace the lid.

The frame can now be chipped away from the brickwork with a hammer and chisel. Take great care when you do this job, since the frames are made of cast-iron and will break easily. If you get it out intact you can re-use it, though if the cover is in a position where it will be run over by vehicles, you will have to change it anyway. Cast-iron covers in this situation must be replaced by steel ones, which are readily obtainable at the builder's merchant. If you expect heavy lorries to run over the cover you will have to go even further and buy a heavy-duty steel cover. Your merchant will be able to advise you.

With the cover and frame removed, it will be easy to see, using the straightedge across two pegs, how much you have to raise or lower the brickwork. You will almost certainly find that the distance is more or less than the thickness of a brick, and this will mean cutting. To cut a brick in half lengthways, the easiest thing to do is to cut off the 'frog'. This is the indentation in the top of the brick. With a brick bolster and club hammer it will come off quite easily and cleanly. You may even find that half a brick is too thick, and in this case you will have to use tiles or even slates.

Use a 3/1 mix of sand and cement to set the bricks, tiles or slates in place, bringing them up to just below the final level as shown by the pegs. Leave the setting of the frame until you have laid the paving right up to the manhole. The frame can then be set to line up with the paving. This will probably not quite line up with the brickwork, and will look somewhat messy. Not to worry, it won't be seen when the inspection cover is in place.

If you have to lower the cover, you will need to knock off the necessary rows of bricks, and may have to put in half a brick or a row of tiles to bring it up to the correct level.

If you want to make the inspection cover really unobtrusive, buy a 'Broads' cover. This consists of a metal frame into which concrete is set. The concrete can be coloured with a colourant powder to match the colour of the paving. When both the concrete and the paving get a little faded and dirty, it will be hardly possible to see the cover.

When the job is completed, make sure you remember to remove the sacking you placed in the hole, and clean it out well.

14 Walling

Walls fulfil many functions in the garden, and in most schemes some walling is desirable. Retaining walls in sloping gardens, boundaries, screens, flower boxes and features can all be built in stone or brick and will add height in an attractive way.

Brick or artificial stone is easier to use than natural stone (with the possible exception of trimmed York-stone) because of its uniform shape. With natural stone, however, because of its informal appearance, a certain amount of leeway in the levels is acceptable.

Brick walls

Bricks can be used in almost any situation. Naturally you should try to choose a brick that harmonizes with its surroundings. If possible, it is obviously desirable to use the same bricks as those used for the house walls, especially if the walling is to be near them. In an older garden, second-hand bricks look more mellow and make a very attractive feature. They can be bought from most demolition contractors. Never use common flettons outside. They are designed primarily for inside walls, and are likely to flake when frosted. If you use sand-faced flettons, note that they have three sides that are treated with a sand finish. It is these sides that are weatherproof, and only they should be seen.

Make the foundations as described previously, tamping down the concrete well and finishing it off so that the top surface is level.

The mortar is made with three parts by volume of soft

builders sand to one part of cement. It is advisable to use a special masonry cement, or to put a proprietary plasticizer in the mixing water. This will make the mortar easier to use, and it will also make the hardened mortar a little more plastic. This means that, if there is a slight movement in the wall due to alternate heating and cooling, the mortar will not crack. If you don't have a plasticizer, a few squirts of washing-up liquid will do much the same job. Make the mix fairly sloppy for bricks.

Again, as for paving, place a spot-board near where you are working to facilitate picking up the mortar. If the walling is next to a paved area, it is a good idea to put a shallow layer of soft sand over the paving near the wall. Any splodges of mortar that fall on it will not then stain, and can be picked up quite easily afterwards.

Start by laying the first brick at one end of a run. Set it with the frog (the depression in the brick) uppermost on a bed of mortar about 2cm(¾in) thick. Tap the brick down with your trowel until there is about 13mm(½in) of mortar under it. Then check it for level, both ways.

Next go to the other end of the run and repeat the process. You will now be able to stretch a bricklayer's line between the two. For the first row or two, I always wrap the line round a spare brick to hold it in place. For subsequent courses, use a bricklayer's line pin stuck in the mortar. Then check that both bricks are aligned. By sandwiching the line between a loose brick on top of the one you have laid, you will be able to position the line so that it runs exactly along the front edge of the brick. If the run is

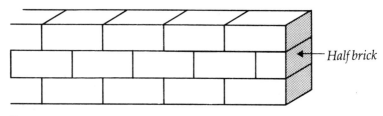

Fig 1. Bonding on a straight run.

very long, you may have to set one or two bricks temporarily in the middle of the run. Using the line as a guide for both line and level, you will be able to lay the first course.

Before butting each brick against the one you have just laid, place a splodge of mortar with the trowel on the two end corners. When the brick is pushed against the last one these two splodges will spread, and no pointing will be necessary afterwards. You may find that putting on the splodge of mortar is a bit of an acquired art, but with a little practice and the right consistency of mortar, you'll quickly get the hang of it.

The second row must be bonded over the first, so that the brick lies with its middle over a joint. If you are building the wall in one single straight run, this will necessitate starting and finishing each alternate row with half a brick.

If, however, you have two or more runs which are set at right-angles to each other, you should lay the first row of the second run before starting on the second course. Since a brick is exactly half as wide as it is long, it is therefore simply a matter of laying the first brick in the row crossways. The illustration makes it quite clear.

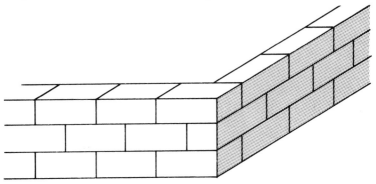

Fig 2. Bonding a right-angle.

As you progress up the wall, check with the spirit level that the bricks are level both ways, and also hold it against the front of the wall to make sure that it is going up straight.

When you reach the top of the wall, a coping must be provided to shed water. This can be done on double-thickness walls by placing a row of bricks on their sides across the wall.

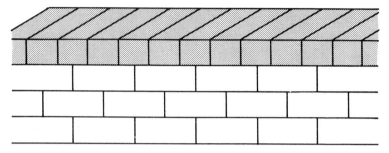

Fig 3. Coping on a double wall.

For a single wall, which is of course too narrow for this, use a special concrete or stone coping about 12.5cm(5in) wide. Set it so that 2.5cm(1in) projects over the face of the brickwork. Alternatively, buy a special bevelled coping which is set so that the apex of the bevel is in the centre of the wall, and projects over the brickwork about 2.5cm(1in) either side.

If the wall is being used to retain soil, it is important to leave weep holes in the first course, to allow water to get away from behind the wall. Otherwise it could soon push it down. Simply leave out half a brick at intervals along the wall, and set in a clay drainage tile. The tile is not in fact necessary, but makes a neater job.

When the mortar is dry but not hard, the wall should be pointed. In fact, with garden walls, it is not necessary to go to the lengths a bricklayer will go to when building a house wall. The simplest way is to wipe over the joints with a piece of wetted sacking to give a neat, flush joint.

Alternatively, cut off the end of a metal bucket handle and use this to rake out the mortar. It will give an attractive, modelled finish.

Taller walls

For a taller wall, for instance one over about 1m(3ft) high, a double row of bricks should be used. This is also necessary if you are using sand-faced flettons where both sides of the wall will be seen and exposed to the elements. Remember that the backs of these bricks are not faced and look ugly, apart from not being weatherproof.

Double walls are built in much the same way except that both sides are built together. The bond is then achieved by placing every other brick across the line of the run, giving much greater strength.

If you are building a tall retaining wall, it will have to withstand a lot of pressure, and here it may be worthwhile building a super-strong construction. This is made by building the two rows with a gap in between. The gap is then filled with concrete to give greater strength. Since the back of the wall will not be seen, this can be made with breeze or concrete blocks. It is as well to tie the two walls together with a builder's butterfly – the twisted wire tie described in the chapter on crazy paving.

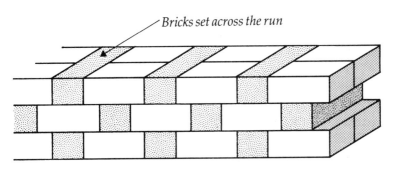

Bricks set across the run

Fig 4. Bonding a solid double wall.

Stone walls

Though many of the techniques are similar for building stone walls, there are certain vital differences. This is mainly due to the fact that stone has a much rougher, more informal surface than brick. For this reason the mortar for stonework must be much drier than that used for bricks. If a little mortar drops onto the face of a brick it will generally fall off, or can easily be flicked off with the point of a trowel. On the rough face of stone it will stick like glue.

Because the mortar is drier, the stones will have to be tapped down with a club hammer, and it will be impossible to make a splodge of mortar stick to the ends as you would with brick. For this reason, it is necessary to point each row of stones before continuing with the rest.

But perhaps the biggest difference is that, because of the uneven face, it is impossible to check that the wall is going up straight by using the spirit level. Still, there are ways and means, and all will be explained later.

Facing stone

Both artificial and natural walling stone can be bought with either a 'cut' or a 'rock' face. A cut face leaves the front of the stone more or less flat, while a rock face makes the front project, giving a less formal and, in my opinion, more attractive finish. Rock-faced stone is more expensive than that with a flat face, because each stone has to be faced. However, it is quite an easy and satisfying job to do yourself.

Start by making a bench. If you have a lot of stone to face, it will be hard on the back if you try to do it crouching down. What you need is a bench that will allow you to work standing up. The ideal height is achieved by placing a paving stone on top of a forty-gallon drum. You should be able to pick one up from a garage or a factory for a pound or so. You'll also need a brick bolster, a club hammer and a straightedge. A straight piece of wood about 4cm × 13mm × 30cm(1½in × ½in × 1ft) is ideal.

Mark a line on the top of the stone, about 13mm(½in) from the face, and chip away the top edge of the stone. Now do the same on both ends, giving yourself a mark to make the line on the other side of the stone. Make sure that the lines chipped away on the ends of the stones are exactly at right-angles to the top, or the wall will not go up straight when you come to building.

1. Walling stone will look better if it is 'faced'. Start by marking a line 13mm (½in) from the face edge.

2. Using a brick bolster and club hammer, chip away the edge along the line you have marked.

3. Now repeat the process on the ends, making sure that the cut is at right angles. Then do the other side.

4. The foundations for the paving should be just a fraction below the level of the paving.

5. When mixing the mortar, make a 3/1 mix of soft sand and cement, using a bucket to measure the quantities.

6. Set the first stones at each end of a run, making sure that it is level with the spirit level.

7. Stretch a tight line along the edge of the stones and hold them in place with a loose stone on top.

8. Now set the remainder of the stones in the run, tapping them down so that they are level and in line with the line.

9. If the wall is to retain soil, weep holes must be left in the bottom course to allow water to escape.

10. If you decide to use 'jumpers', they must be set after the remainder of the course. Remove one stone.

11. The jumpers are made the same length as the stones but twice the height, so they will fit into the space.

12. The jumper must be levelled independently, making sure that it is perfectly level both ways.

13. Once the first course is laid, it must be pointed in with mortar before the second course is set on top.

14. The top of the wall should be finished with a coping stone which projects a little over the front of the wall.

15. When the mortar is dry but not hard, it should be pointed by raking it back with a short piece of wood.

16. If any mortar has fallen on the face of the stone, it should be removed afterwards, with a wire brush.

102

Building

When you are ready to start, set the first two stones at each end of the run, in the way described for bricks. The brick-layer's line is then set to run along the line you have cut when you faced the stone. As you set each stone, check with the spirit level that it is level both ways. This should ensure that the wall goes up straight, but it is worthwhile standing back and sighting along the wall after each run is set. If you have a good eye you will easily see any mistakes. If not, bang a straight stake at the end of each run, level it with the spirit level so that it is perfectly upright, and sight the wall against it.

When each course is laid, it will have to be pointed by working mortar in between the stones with the edge of a pointing trowel. Leave it rough at the front for the time being. When the wall is completed, or before you finish for the evening, the rough mortar at the face of the wall should be raked out with a piece of wood, to leave it recessed about 13mm(½in).

Some manufacturers will supply 'jumpers'. These are stones made twice the thickness of the main body of stones, and they should be set in the wall here and there to give an attractive random effect. To ensure that they don't interfere with the bricklayer's line, they must be set when the remainder of the course is finished, and levelled with the next course.

As with brickwork, the final job is to set a coping stone on the top of the wall. These can generally be bought with the walling, and are cut to size. If you have faced the walling stone, these will also have to be faced, and they should be trimmed so that each stone is exactly the same width. Again, set them so that the front of the coping overhangs the wall.

Examine the wall carefully when you have finished. If there is any mortar stuck to the face, brush it off with a wire brush. It should come off cleanly if your mortar was dry enough.

Piers

Brick or stone walls can be simply finished 'straight' or they can be finished off with a pier. This provides a logical and definitive finish to a run of walling, and adds strength. For walls over about 1m(3ft) high, they should be considered necessary. Piers are also necessary if you intend to hang a gate in a run of walling. The constant use of even a small gate will place quite a stress on the wall. For added strength, the piers can be filled with concrete, or they can be left hollow, filled with a suitable compost and planted up to make an attractive feature.

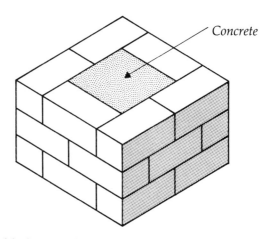

Concrete

Fig 5. For added strength piers can be filled with concrete.

The dimensions of the pier should be such that constant cutting of bricks is eliminated. This means that the smallest pier will be 1½ bricks wide. This is really rather too small. A better size is 2½ bricks wide.

As with straight walling, make the foundation twice the size of the finished pier. Naturally, if the pier is to add strength to the wall, it must be built with it, so that the wall keys into it.

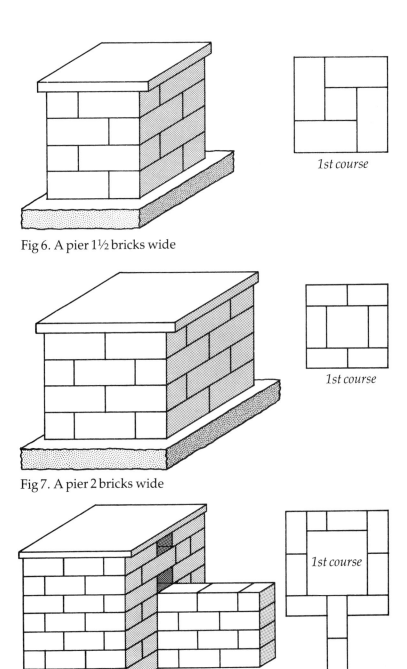

1st course

Fig 6. A pier 1½ bricks wide

1st course

Fig 7. A pier 2 bricks wide

1st course

Fig 8. Keying a wall into the pier

The bricks or stones are set in much the same way as described for straight brickwork. The only difference is that, since the runs are too short to use a bricklayer's line, the stones are levelled in with a spirit level.

If you intend to hang a gate on the pier, don't forget to set the necessary fittings in the brickwork as you build.

Arches

The building of an archway should not be approached lightly. This is quite a skilled operation, but with care, the competent handyman can make a good job.

The brickwork forming the archway is fashioned around a wooden template, which supports the bricks until the mortar is hard, when it can be removed and the arch will be self-supporting.

Make the template as shown in the drawing, using stout timbers and hardboard or plywood. This is set up in the space left for the arch, and temporarily fixed to the brick-

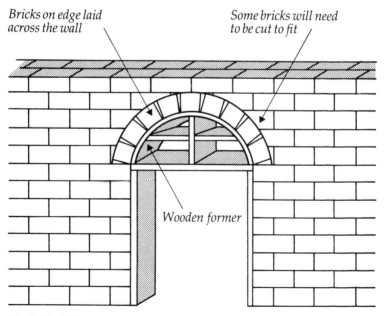

Bricks on edge laid across the wall

Some bricks will need to be cut to fit

Wooden former

Fig 9. Building an archway using a wooden former.

work with nails driven into the mortar. Leave the nails pro-
jecting a little from the timber, so that they can be easily
withdrawn when you remove the template.

When the curved part of the arch is reached, the bricks
are set across the line of the brickwork, and on edge to give
added strength. Building then continues normally, cutting
the bricks in to meet the curve as you come to it.

It will be seen that this method of building is only suitable for walls 23cm(9in) wide, and will not work on
11.5cm(4½in) walls. Indeed, arches should not be attemp-
ted in walling less than 23cm(9in) wide.

Once the mortar is hard, the template can be removed
and the arch will be self-suporting.

15 Steps

In steeply sloping gardens, steps are a necessity. But they should not be considered purely utilitarian. Well designed and built, they can make a very attractive feature in themselves. But, as with paths, they should never be skimped even if they are designed to be purely practical. If they are too narrow, or too steep, they will make the remainder of the garden appear smaller, upsetting the scale of the overall scheme. Obviously the width of steps will vary according to the design and size of the garden, but you should aim to make them at least 1.2m(4ft) wide.

The depth of the treads (the flat part of the step) should also be fairly generous – never less than 45cm(18in). The height of the risers – the upright part – will vary according to the difference in height between the lower and upper levels that the steps join. It is important, though, to make them neither too low, when they are un-noticeable and can constitute a dangerous 'trip', or too high, making them difficult and tiring to climb. Ideally, they should be 12–15cm(5–6in).

Before you start setting out the steps, some careful planning is necessary. You need to decide how many steps you'll need, and how high the risers must be. Start by determining the distance between the top and bottom levels. Get somebody to hold the straightedge at the top level, and make sure it is level with the spirit level. Then drop a tape from the bottom of the straightedge to the bottom level to ascertain the difference in height.

Each step is to be between 12 and 15cm(5–6in) high, so the distance between the two levels should be divided by this amount to give the number of steps required. For example, if the difference in height was, say, 41cm(16½in) three steps, each 13.8cm(5½in) high, would be required. If the treads are to be 45cm(18in) deep, then allowing for an overlap of 2.5cm(1in) on each step, they will take up 127cm(4ft 3in) in length.

Start building at the bottom of the flight. Put in a concrete foundation, and set on this a course of bricks or stone. The height of the foundation takes a bit of head scratching too. If the riser is to be 15cm(6in) high, and you are working with bricks and paving slabs, work it out like this. The slab is 5cm(2in) thick. Allow for 13mm(½in) of mortar underneath this, making 6.3cm(2½in). The brick is 7.5cm(3in) thick and this will need another 13mm(½in) of mortar underneath it, making 15cm(6in) in all. So, the concrete foundation should come flush with the bottom level. If you only wanted the riser to be 12cm(5in) high, you would have to drop the concrete foundation by 2.5cm(1in) below the bottom level.

1. Start by setting a single course of stone as the bottom 'riser' of the steps.

With the bricks set, you can now dig out behind them and fill in with concrete, to make a base for the paving slab treads. Set these on the bricks, leaving an overlap at the front of about 2.5cm(1in). At the back of the paving slabs,

2. When this is set, dig out behind it, low enough to allow a concrete base just below the level of the stone.

3. Using a dryish mix of ballast and cement, lay the base, making sure it is not above the riser level.

dig out the foundation for the second riser and make the second step in the same way. Bear in mind that, if the top step is to meet the lawn, the slabs should be a little below the grass level to allow for easy mowing.

4. Put a layer of mortar along the riser, and lay the slab on three mounds of cement mortar.

5. The slab should now be levelled so that it slopes very slightly towards the front.

6. Set the remainder of the slabs for the 'tread', and then fill behind them to form the base for the second riser.

7. This is now set just behind the first tread. The soil is then dug out behind and another step built.

16 Plants

However attractive your paving slabs may be, and however well they have been laid, they will still tend to look a little 'hard' in the garden setting. There's no doubt about it, hard landscaping of any sort needs plants to soften it. Chosen well, plants will also add a great deal of colour and interest to an otherwise barren area, and they will thrive with little or no attention.

Walls, too, can be brightened up with the addition of plants. It is quite surprising how little some alpine plants need for survival, and many will live happily stuck in a crevice in a wall, with no apparent means of sustenance. Not only will they grow – they'll thrive.

Obviously with paving, and walls too to a lesser extent, the place for planting must be carefully chosen. Leave clear the area that will get the most use. Plant those subjects that will put up with a little maltreatment where they may get trodden on or kicked, and leave the tenderer plants where they can enjoy a little peace and quiet to get on with their job.

Even without planting in the paving or walling, the area can be livened up with tubs and troughs of annual plants and walls can be decorated with pots and hanging baskets.

Obviously then, the first thing to do is to get to know your plants – which plants will do well, and where they will flourish. I have suggested a few here, but I would strongly recommend that you look out a good book on alpine and rockery plants and another on conifers before making your final choice. The great range of suitable plants is much too numerous to describe here.

Plants for crevices

Many alpine and rock plants can be grown in tiny crevices in walls and in paving. If you intend to plant a wall, leave a few spaces unpointed here and there and fill them with a little ordinary garden soil. They will also grow well in spaces left between natural paving. But if you wish to grow them between artificial slabs (which butt much closer together), simply chip off a corner where you want the plants to go, when you are laying the slabs. They will look unfinished and ugly until they are planted, but will reward your patience well when they grow. Work a little soil into the hole and push it down under the slabs. That will be plenty for most small plants.

Alyssum saxatile is the popular small, perennial alyssum. It is especially useful in walls, where it will tumble down, covering quite a large area. In the spring it is covered with a mass of bright yellow flowers. A common plant, but not to be scorned.

1. *Alyssum saxatile.*

2. *Aubrietia* on a wall.

Arabis, or rock cress, is another fairly common inhabitant of British gardens, and with good reason. It forms tufts of bright-green foliage covered in bright-pink or white flowers. A worthy plant for paved areas where it will not get a lot of rough treatment. This one can tend to get a bit straggly after a few years, so you may wish to replace it.

Aubrietia is another trailing plant that will do well in walls or in paving where it can be protected from pedestrian traffic. Again, it makes its show in the springtime, and its bright pink, blue, crimson, purple or lilac flowers make a striking contrast to *Alyssum saxatile*. This one, too, may get a little leggy after a few years and benefits from being trimmed back a little after flowering.

Potentilla aurea plena is a beauty for planting in paving, though it will not tolerate a lot of harsh treatment. It forms small hummocks of glossy green leaves that look bright and cheerful most of the year, but it is at its best in the spring, when it is covered with double yellow flowers.

The *Saxifrages* and *Sedums* are two very large groups of plants, most of which can be grown between paving slabs and in walls. There is a great variety of colour in these two families, but the foliage alone would warrant them a place. *Sempervivums* are another large group. Often known as houseleeks, they will live almost anywhere. I have seen dozens of them growing quite happily on tiled roofs where there is no apparent source of nourishment at all. They form rosettes of foliage that vary from the tiny, hairy spider houseleek to types with large, glossy, fleshy leaves. Their flowers too are varied, though even without flowers at all they make an attractive show and are a fascinating collector's plant.

Thymus, or thyme, is well known as a culinary herb, and of course can be planted in the paving to form a useful as well as decorative addition. But here again there are many, varied forms, with green, yellow, silver and variegated foliage and white or purple flowers. They can be planted where they will receive a little wear, because, when lightly bruised, they give off the most delicious, aromatic fragrance. Three distinct advantages with this family and definitely not to be missed.

3. *Sempervivum* growing from a wall crevice.

Larger plants

If you wish to grow larger plants in a paved area special provision will have to be made for them when laying the paving. In areas that will receive no use you can leave out quite large planting areas. These will add height and interest and will break up what may otherwise be a monotonous stretch of stone. Also, leave out the odd slab, or half a slab, here and there where taller plants will not be in the way.

When the paving has set hard, knock out the concrete base below the planting hole and fill it with compost (John Innes No. 3 potting compost is best). Don't use garden soil in the holes for the larger plants, since they will require better conditions than the alpines and rock plants. Of course, in larger areas left in the paving, almost anything will go, but in the isolated holes, conifers with a prostrate habit are definitely to be preferred.

There are several varieties of conifer that will grow very close to the ground and will spread along it, hugging the paving. These are ideal, because they can be trimmed back as you wish.

4. *Juniperus horizontalis.*

117

The junipers are probably the best of this type of low growing conifer, and there are several attractive forms.

Juniperus communis depressa, or Canadian juniper, forms a large, spreading mat of green stems and leaves, silver beneath and turning bronze in winter. It likes full sun and is one of the best for the purpose.

Juniperus communis effusa has green leaves, silvery beneath, and this one stays green in winter to make a pleasant contrast to the Canadian juniper.

Juniperus horizontalis, the creeping juniper, has a number of good forms, the leaves of which are greyish blue. Two of the best forms are *J.h.montana* and *J.h.wiltonii*.

Juniperus sabina has some useful forms for paving planting, though some of them will grow a little higher and should therefore be used only on larger areas. *J.s.cupressifolia* is a good, low-growing, green form, while *J.s.tamariscifolia* will grow a little higher, making a spreading, flat-topped bush of emerald green.

There are, of course, many other conifers and other types of plants suitable for growing in walls and paving. Generally, your local nurseryman will be able to advise.

5. *Juniperus sabina tamariscifolia.*

Growing in containers

One of the best ways of brightening up the patio, or that rather boring wall, is to grow plants in containers. With a collection of suitable containers, a succession of annual plants can be grown that will give colour through all the months of the year in which you are likely to use your patio.

Fill them with annuals and keep moving them around to show them off to their best advantage. Of course, containers can be planted with perennials, but unless you use alpines and rock plants and a few dwarf conifers they never give the same amount of colour as do annuals.

Start by selecting containers that will suit the situation. Make sure they have adequate drainage holes and start filling by putting in a generous layer of drainage material. Broken pots, builder's rubble or gravel will all do the job. Then fill them with John Innes No. 3 potting compost. Don't use one of the newer soil-less composts, because they dry out too quickly and are difficult to water.

Start in the spring or early summer with summer bedding plants. Geraniums, fuchsias, petunias, salvias, alyssum and lobelia all look fine in containers. These are pulled out when the first frosts cut them down, and are replaced with spring bulbs, wallflowers, sweet-williams, pansies, forget-me-nots and the like. Try to avoid the taller growing plants, especially bulbs which have tender stems and will not stand up to exposure.

The same plants can be used in hanging baskets which can be fixed to walls with a hook plugged into the brickwork. Special 'half-baskets' are available and these are particularly suitable for walls.

The one golden rule with tubs, troughs and hanging baskets is 'Don't forget them'. Bear in mind that they will dry out faster than plants in the open ground, and the only source of water and food they have is what you give them. Forget them, and they will suffer quickly. Remember them, and they will reward you well.

17 Aftercare

One of the beauties of stonework is that once it's down it requires little or no maintenance. All that's needed for the most part is a broom! There are, however, one or two jobs to do occasionally in certain circumstances.

1. One of the advantages of paved areas is that most of the maintenance can be done with a broom.

However careful you may be with paving, it is quite likely that one or two slabs will 'rock' after a while. This is generally a fault in the laying, but even the best paviors are guilty of the odd one or two now and again.

If the slabs have been butted up close together, it is almost impossible to lift them in order to relay. The cracks between the slabs are too small to allow a spade to be forced down between them to lift the offending slab. In this case the way out is to hammer a small wedge of wood between the slabs to prevent them rocking. Certainly, the wood will rot away in time, but by then enough dust and dirt should have worked down between the slabs to hold them firm.

Algae and moss will grow on damp stone, and this, although encouraged on garden walls because it mellows the brick or stone, is to be avoided on paving. Algal growth in particular will make the slabs slippery and potentially very dangerous. Both algae and moss are, of course plants, so they can be killed with an appropriate chemical. The cheapest is probably tar oil, used normally to kill overwintering eggs of insects on trees and shrubs. It is also very effective in killing moss and algae. There are also several proprietary formulations made specifically for the job, but these tend to be more expensive and no more effective.

Pointing in walls may become dislodged due to frost action. Here, the mortar must be raked right out of the wall to provide a 'key' for new pointing, and the space refilled with mortar made as before. Don't repoint when the weather is frosty or the new pointing will be affected in the same way.

Perhaps one of the biggest problems in paving is weed growth. No matter how closely the slabs are butted, or even if they are pointed in between, weeds, particularly grass, somehow seem to get a hold. It looks unsightly and can also be slippery. Though weeds can be scraped out with a knife, it is a laborious and time-consuming job, and will not prevent new seeds blowing in to start growing all over again. Undoubtedly, the best way to control weeds in paths and paving is by the use of chemicals.

2. Remove algae by watering with tar oil, and weeds with a weedkiller.

One of the cheapest chemicals to give total control of weeds in paving is sodium chlorate. But this has two disadvantages. Firstly, there is some fire risk, though the chemical is now generally sold with a fire-depressant in the formulation. More risk perhaps lies in causing damage to the plants that edge the paving. Sodium chlorate will 'creep' through the soil, and could well damage plants some way away from where it was applied.

Better are the newer total weedkillers which contain simazine. These will not only kill the weeds that are there, but will also prevent new seeds from germinating. Simazine will not 'creep' through the soil, but great care must be taken to ensure that it does not come into contact with the foiliage of plants you wish to keep.

The only other chore that will have to be seen to regularly is the feeding and watering of plants. Alpines and rock plants require very little fertilizer, and should be left alone unless they appear to be suffering. Conifers growing in spaces left in the paving will need feeding, and this should be done with a proprietary rose fertilizer early in the spring.

Plants growing in tubs, troughs and baskets will need regular watering. Generally, annual plants will need no feeding after they have been planted. All this does is to produce lush growth of the leaves and stems at the expense of flowers. A dressing of general fertilizer incorporated into the compost before planting will be sufficient, generally, to last them through their lives. Again, feeding should be carried out if the plants appear to be suffering.

3. Plants in tubs and troughs will need regular watering and feeding if they are to give of their best.

Glossary

Aggregate – A mixture of sand and gravel used to make concrete.

Algae – Tiny plants that grow on cold, damp places, forming a green slime.

Alpines – Plants that are native to mountain habitats.

Annual – A plant that is raised from seed, flowers and dies in the same year.

Bolster – A wide cold chisel used for cutting brick or stone.

Bonding – The practice of setting bricks so that joints do not correspond on alternate rows.

Butterfly – A wire frame shaped like a butterfly's wings, used to join two walls together.

Compasses – A drawing instrument used to make circles.

Coping – The capping of a wall used to prevent the entry of water.

Course – A row of bricks or stone in a wall.

Cure – To ensure that concrete dries slowly, giving added strength.

Damp-proof course (DPC) – A membrane of waterproof material set in a house wall to prevent rising damp.

Drainage tile – An earthenware pipe used for land drainage.

Engineering brick – A brick made of hard material used where excess loads are expected, or where frost would damage softer materials.

Face – The front of a brick or stone

Fat – A mixture of fine sand, cement and water, worked to the surface of concrete when tamped down.

Fillet – A narrow strip of cement left when pointing paving.

Fletton – A cheaply made brick used for interior walls.

Footings – Concrete foundations of a wall.

Former – A metal beam used for shuttering deep concrete.

French curve – A drawing instrument used for making curves.

General fertilizer – An artificial plant food containing the three major plant nutrients.

Gulley – An earthenware pot used to trap water and transfer it to the drainage system.

Hardcore – Any hard material, such as bricks or broken concrete, used in the base of driveways or paving.

Herbicide – A chemical weedkiller.

Inspection cover – The metal lid used to cover a hole made for inspecting drains and sewers.

Masonry cement – Special cement containing a plasticizer.

Mortar – A mixture of sand and cement used in bricklaying and paving.

Organic matter – Plant or animal debris that will rot down in the soil to form humus.

Perennial – A permanent plant that, though it may die down in winter, will flower year after year.

Plasterer's float – A wooden or metal float used to apply plaster.

Plasticizer – A cement additive that makes concrete more plastic and flexible.

Pointing – Filling in between bricks or slabs with mortar.

Portland cement – 'Ordinary' cement without additives.

Radius – The distance from the centre to the edge of a circle.

Random – An unplanned pattern of paving.

Retaining wall – A wall used to hold back soil.

Riven – Natural stone cut by hand, leaving a textured surface.

Roofing square – A large metal square used by roofers.

Sand-faced fletton – A cheap brick with a weatherproof face.

Sharp sand – A gritty sand used where strength is important.

Shuttering – A temporary retainer for concrete.

Soft sand – A soft, clay sand used for brickwork and paving.

Spirit level – A tool for ascertaining levels.

Stable blocks – Small, black, square blocks, traditionally used in stable yards.

Subsoil – The soil underlying the topsoil, generally not suitable for growing plants.

Weep hole – A hole in a retaining wall, allowing the escape of water.

Index

128